THE BRONFENBRENNER PRIMER

This is the first ever introduction to Urie Bronfenbrenner's Ecological Systems Framework written specifically for undergraduate students. The author provides a carefully structured, guided introduction to Bronfenbrenner's concepts, their interpretation, and their potential applications. Bronfenbrenner's scientific analysis of the role the environment plays in human development earned him a premier place alongside Jean Piaget, Sigmund Freud, and Erik Erikson as a contributor to our understanding of developmental processes. His ideas are essential for analyzing how development happens, how it goes astray, how to right it when it does, and how to create environments that will promote healthy development.

The Bronfenbrenner Primer walks students through each component of the framework in a logical order, helping students build a solid, systematic understanding. It describes the background and context that led Bronfenbrenner to develop his framework, illustrates a wide array of potential applications, and provides activities students can do to practice applying the framework to their own experience. Honed over 25 years of teaching Bronfenbrenner's ideas, this text will be essential reading for students across the behavioral and social sciences.

Lawrence G. Shelton is a Developmental Psychologist who has taught in the Human Development and Family Studies Program at the University of Vermont since 1971. He has taught and applied Bronfenbrenner's ideas in novel ways for the past 25 years in a wide-ranging teaching and consulting career. Shelton has elaborated on and expanded Bronfenbrenner's ideas to emphasize the necessity of integrating ecological and developmental perspectives, an approach he refers to as Develecology.

THE BRONFENBRENNER PRIMER

A Guide to Develecology

Lawrence G. Shelton

Routledge
Taylor & Francis Group

NEW YORK AND LONDON

First published 2019
by Routledge
711 Third Avenue, New York, NY 10017

and by Routledge
2 Park Square, Milton Park, Abingdon, Oxon, OX14 4RN

Routledge is an imprint of the Taylor & Francis Group, an informa business

Library of Congress Cataloging-in-Publication Data
Names: Shelton, Lawrence G., author.
Title: The Bronfenbrenner primer : a guide to develecology /
Lawrence G. Shelton.
Description: New York, NY : Routledge, 2018. | Includes
bibliographical references and index.
Identifiers: LCCN 2018006571 | ISBN 9781138037151 (hbk : alk. paper)
| ISBN 9781138037168 (pbk : alk. paper) | ISBN 9781315136066 (ebk)
Subjects: LCSH: Bronfenbrenner, Urie, 1917-2005. | Developmental
psychology. | Environmental psychology. | Social ecology.
Classification: LCC BF713 .S5147 2018 | DDC 155–dc23
LC record available at https://lccn.loc.gov/2018006571

ISBN: 978-1-138-03715-1 (hbk)
ISBN: 978-1-138-03716-8 (pbk)
ISBN: 978-1-315-13606-6 (ebk)

Typeset in Bembo
by Wearset Ltd, Boldon, Tyne and Wear

I respectfully dedicate this work to
Urie Bronfenbrenner (1917–2005)
Armin Grams (1924–2002)
and all of their generation on whose work we build

CONTENTS

PREFACE

A primer is a book presenting the basic elements of a subject, intended for beginning students. *The Bronfenbrenner Primer* is intended to help you understand one of the core topics in the study of human development—the framework of Urie Bronfenbrenner's Ecological Systems Model of Development. I wrote this guide for my students at the University of Vermont. Now I am pleased to provide it to a wider audience. It is particularly gratifying for me to have it appear in 2018, the 101st anniversary of Urie Bronfenbrenner's birth.

This book is not an attempt to present and explain Bronfenbrenner's extensive body of work, or the development of his thinking across his career. It is neither a critique of his model nor a comparison of his thinking to other theories of development. I will not assess the current state of research using his framework. I intend only to provide an introductory guide to understanding the ecological framework for development proposed by Urie Bronfenbrenner, as published in his 1979 book, *The Ecology of Human Development*. In his book, Bronfenbrenner presented a scientific analysis of the role the environment plays in human development. That book and his subsequent writing on the topic earned Bronfenbrenner a premier place as a contributor to our understanding of human development. His work is cited in every developmental textbook, along with the views of Sigmund Freud, Erik Erikson, Jean Piaget, and others who shape our conceptions of development.

I teach to help students construct an understanding of how people develop. Why does development occur, and how? What influences the course of development? If you want to facilitate development, how can you do that? Over the course of my career, I have studied the works of Freud, Erikson, Sullivan, Piaget, and many other researchers and theorists who consider the processes of development. Each is useful to some degree for understanding some aspects of development. While all of these and many other approaches assume that the **environment** is a significant determinant of the course or content of development, it is a challenge to find serious consideration of *how* context shapes development. What are the processes involved? What characteristics of the environment are important in development? How do we compare environments to understand how they lead to differences in development?

As a practitioner, an *applied developmental psychologist*, who tries to address barriers to development and to promote development, I need to understand not only how people develop, but how the environment shapes development. I need to know what changes in the environment will support development. I have to try to use both a *developmental perspective* and an *ecological perspective* to grasp how development has been shaped by the environment and what changes in the environment might shape development in desirable directions.

Bronfenbrenner provides a conceptual framework for understanding the environment half of the processes of development. His framework has been essential to my understanding and my work for many years. The classic and current theorists and researchers of development form one strong core of our understanding, but it was incomplete until Bronfenbrenner's work provided a way to conceptualize the environments in which development must occur. This second core is necessary to provide the *dual perspective needed* to analyze how development happens, how it goes astray, how to right it, and how to create environments that will promote healthy development. Fundamentally, development is the process of transacting with and adapting to the environment we experience as we change biologically.

Over the years, as I taught and practiced, the dual perspectives of development and ecology became so integrated in my thinking, that I eventually coined the term *develecology* to refer to the study of the relationship between development and the ecosystem in which it occurs. Thus, this book also serves as an introduction to the study of develecology.

While Bronfenbrenner's framework became essential to my thinking, and central to our curriculum in Human Development and Family Studies at the University of Vermont, I became convinced of its power as a tool for organizing our thinking about development and the contexts in which it occurs. I also grew more aware that the framework is not well explained in the developmental texts I used and reviewed, and that it is not as widely or deeply incorporated in training or in practice as I believe it should be.

Bronfenbrenner's framework is a challenge for beginning students, but they can grasp it and learn to apply it. They often find it so useful in later graduate study and in professional work that they are surprised so few people know it or use it. Learning Bronfenbrenner's scheme helps students cross the bridge from a focus on subjective experience to becoming critical thinkers who can learn and use formal theories of development. It allows them to think systemically about complex aspects of development, relationships, families, social institutions, and policy. Those who understand it are able to conceptualize influences on development as well as approaches to changing ecosystems that hinder development so as to reduce problems (Shelton, 2012).

I developed this book through two decades of teaching Bronfenbrenner's framework to first- and second-year students at the University of Vermont. Those hundreds of students helped me understand Bronfenbrenner's scheme and learn to explain and apply it. My interpretations of Bronfenbrenner's scheme in this book are firmly rooted in Bronfenbrenner's own explanations of his thinking. The examples, explanations, and illustrations here evolved through my attempts to help students understand and apply the concepts consistently, and are mine. Any departures from Bronfenbrenner's meaning and intent are my responsibility. I hope I have explicated his ideas, and not misrepresented them. My students have found the explanations helpful, as I hope you will. I hope you also find the book, Bronfenbrenner's perspective, and develecology useful.

References

Bronfenbrenner, U. (1979). *The Ecology of Human Development: Experiments by Nature and Design*. Cambridge, MA: Harvard University Press.

Shelton, L. G. (2012, Summer). An introductory family science course built on Bronfenbrenner's ecological framework. *NCFR Report, Family Focus on Teaching Family Science*, 57.2, pp. 20–22.

ACKNOWLEDGMENTS

This book is for my students in Human Development and Family Studies and others like them who want to understand the ecological concepts put forth by Urie Bronfenbrenner and to apply them in analyzing social settings as contexts for human development. I am grateful to the late Professor Armin Grams who introduced me to Bronfenbrenner's ecology and led the way in helping our

FIGURE 0.1   Urie Bronfenbrenner

students learn to use it. I deeply appreciate the editorial contributions of my wife, Lauren Shelton, and Graduate Teaching Fellow *Extraordinaire*, Devon Voake.

I thank the many hundreds of students who have shaped my understanding of Bronfenbrenner's framework, develecology, and this book. Neither the students nor I would have learned nearly as much without the gentle and thoughtful assistance of Hillary Hazan Glass, Angela Albeck, Julie Leaf, Talia Glesner, Sarah Shackett, Devon Voake, and Simrat Peltier.

Writing the book was facilitated by a sabbatical leave provided by the University of Vermont.

The illustrations in this book were conceived by the author and executed by Ellen Voorheis.

Illustrations © Lawrence G. Shelton and used by permission.

Thanks to Harvard University Press for permission to reprint excerpts from *The Ecology of Human Development: Experiments by Nature and Design* by Urie Bronfenbrenner (Cambridge, MA: Harvard University Press), Copyright © 1979 by the President and Fellows of Harvard College.

1

INTRODUCTION TO URIE BRONFENBRENNER

Who Was Urie Bronfenbrenner?

Urie Bronfenbrenner was a developmental psychologist. He earned a doctorate at the University of Michigan, and then taught for many years in the Department of Human Development at Cornell University. Bronfenbrenner wanted research on child development to be understood and to be useful. He especially wanted public policy to focus on supporting the development of children and families so that all children would have opportunity to grow up healthy and competent. He strongly advocated for Lyndon Johnson's "war" against poverty, and helped to design and implement the Head Start program for children from low-income families.

As Bronfenbrenner's career progressed, he became increasingly frustrated by the lack of child development research that could be used directly to understand how development was influenced by the neighborhood and community children lived in and how social policy affected the environments that shaped children's development. As he argued vigorously for research that considered the environment as well as the development that happened within it, he came to understand that one reason researchers didn't pay specific attention to the environment was that the developmental sciences didn't actually have a way of *conceptualizing* the environment. Although professionals in the field talked about the importance of the environment, and referred to the ecology of children and families, there was no common language or conceptual framework for identifying the elements of the ecosystem or how it affected development or relationships.

Researchers often measured or gathered data on characteristics of people, such as social class, family income, education, race, or ethnicity, measures we refer to as demographic data. But these data don't really reflect the environments people live in, what people do, where they spend their time, or who the important people in their lives are. Demographic measures don't tell us how the environment treats people. Bronfenbrenner began to refer to the typical demographic variables as people's "social addresses," measures that tell us where people live in the social system. He wanted to see research that actually assessed what people experienced in the social system, what the characteristics of their specific environments were. From these, he hoped, we could learn how the environment acts in shaping development.

Bronfenbrenner came to ecology early. His understanding of the world was deeply affected in childhood, when, as he described in the Preface to his 1979 book, he had the good fortune to grow up on the grounds of a state institution for people with intellectual and psychiatric disabilities. There he roamed the fields and the woods with his father, a neuropathologist, trained in medicine. His father also had a Ph.D. in zoology, and Bronfenbrenner described him as a "field naturalist at heart" (1979, p. xi). He wrote: "Wherever we were he would alert my unobservant eyes to the workings of nature by pointing to the functional interdependence between living organisms and their surroundings" (1979, p. xii).

What Did Urie Bronfenbrenner Do?

Bronfenbrenner realized psychology did not have ecological concepts adequate for answering the kinds of questions he asked, questions that were necessary for understanding how society hindered development and how we might change it to support development. So he set out to create a way to conceptualize the human ecosystems in which development occurs. He set forth the framework in his 1979 book, *The Ecology of Human Development*. In the book, he outlined the concepts he distilled from decades of research and theory about what influences human development. He specified the concepts that were to be included (Definitions), offered a few assumptions that were important to make (Propositions), and presented a set of testable Hypotheses about how the ecosystem functions in shaping development. He created a scientific conceptualization, with as much specificity, objectivity, and clarity as possible. He encouraged researchers to test it, revise it, and expand on it, as these are the basic principles of any science. Bronfenbrenner continued to revise, test, and expand his understanding of development throughout his long career.

For his framework, Bronfenbrenner assumed a constructivist model of development, with the person an active participant in experience, and attempting to make sense of it. In the process of exploring and trying to adapt to the environment, the person constructs an understanding of the environment, and acquires skills to deal with it. Bronfenbrenner drew many ideas from Jean Piaget, particularly Piaget's book *The Construction of Reality in the Child* (1954).

In trying to capture the essence of the ecosystem, Bronfenbrenner began with the work of Kurt Lewin, who had tackled the task decades earlier. Acknowledging his debt to Lewin, Bronfenbrenner wrote:

> the conception of the environment as a set of regions each contained within the next draws heavily on the theories of Kurt Lewin (1931, 1935, 1938). Indeed, this work may be viewed as an attempt to provide psychological and sociological substance to Lewin's brilliantly conceived topological territories.
>
> *(1979, p. 9; for more detail about Bronfenbrenner's understanding of Lewin, see Bronfenbrenner's 1977 article)*

To these beginnings, Bronfenbrenner added concepts and connections drawn from a wide array of social science research to formulate his framework for putting development in context.

Why Is Bronfenbrenner's Work Important to Me?

As an undergraduate at Harvard, I majored in a field called "Social Relations." The title referred not to college party life, but to understanding human development and relationships within their social contexts. Social Relations was an interdisciplinary department incorporating developmental, social, and clinical psychologists, cultural anthropologists, sociologists, and psychiatrists. I studied Freud, Erikson, Piaget, Sullivan, Lewin, and Skinner, and was exposed to psychophysiology, psychopathology, psycholinguistics, anthropology, sociology, and more. My subsequent career and teaching have evolved from the integrative, multidisciplinary, and applied foundation that was laid down during those undergraduate years. I went on to study Child Psychology at the University of Minnesota. Studying child psychology research, I was often frustrated by two shortcomings in the professional literature. First, much of the research was not really developmental, because it studied age differences, not change over time. Cross-sectional studies can't really identify the processes or course of development in the way that longitudinal studies can. Second, research often ignored the context of the subjects in the studies, the environments that children were in. I was greatly pleased to hear Bronfenbrenner express his own similar dissatisfactions with the field.

When I began to study and then to teach Bronfenbrenner's framework, I found that it fit neatly onto the multidisciplinary foundation I began to develop in my major in Social Relations. His concepts provided me a language for describing professional as well as personal experiences I had had in a variety of programs and institutional settings. As a developmental psychologist myself, and a professor of Human Development and Family Studies, I was familiar with the problems in our fields he was responding to. Most importantly, his framework filled a gap in my understanding of development, the gap he had identified as the lack of a conceptual language to describe how people and our environments interact in the processes of development.

As I worked to help students understand this conceptual language, I gradually discovered how powerful and essential Bronfenbrenner's concepts really are. Learning and being able to apply the framework can make a person's understanding of the ecosystem and of development significantly more valid, differentiated, and useful. Bronfenbrenner provides a general, and generalizable, framework that can guide both individual attempts to facilitate development and analysis of policy and proposed social interventions. Bronfenbrenner's approach *applies to all development*, optimal and less than optimal. It applies equally to children developing competence and adolescents becoming delinquents or addicts. Increasingly, I have found Bronfenbrenner's work consistent with the central features of the theories that have survived best.

Bronfenbrenner's views have become a major organizing scheme in my understanding of development and relationships. As I have evolved into an applied develecologist, his ideas have become essential in my teaching. As his ideas have become so important to my understanding of development, I have been increasingly puzzled by the relative inattention to Bronfenbrenner's perspective in the texts available for use in courses in human development. His ideas are usually mentioned, sometimes accurately, but they rarely are used to organize the material in texts.

I think one reason scant attention has been paid to Bronfenbrenner's work outside the research community is that his primary presentation of the framework, in his 1979 book *The Ecology of Human Development*, appeared now nearly four decades ago and was addressed to graduate students and researchers. The presentation of the perspective appearing there is tied to analyses of research studies that are now dated. As well, the terminology Bronfenbrenner uses is rich and precise, able to be understood and appreciated only with considerable study. So, while his views are recognized as important and provocative, and are mentioned in nearly every human development text, they are given cursory treatment, usually only in outline form. Typically, his views are presented as one of several viewpoints or approaches to understanding development, and then are not integrated with the material on development that follows. This treatment gives students the impression that Bronfenbrenner is as important and irrelevant as Freud and other outdated theorists mentioned in the introductory chapters, and thus worthy of being forever after ignored. This impression is misleading, of course, since the classic theories provide concepts that have gained wide acceptance in modern culture. The classic notions of old theories of development, behavior, and relationships form the historic underpinnings of the social sciences.

We cannot understand our current thinking if we can't place it in its intellectual context. In my view, Bronfenbrenner's ideas deserve close study and understanding because they incorporate concepts essential to our useful interpretation of human development. There has been no introduction to his views, nothing published that makes his perspective accessible to students. This primer is my attempt to fill that gap, to present the human developmental ecological approach of Bronfenbrenner in an accessible manner, to put this powerful tool in the hands of students and others who would understand development.

References

Bronfenbrenner, U. (1977). Lewinian space and ecological substance. *Journal of Social Issues*, 32, 513–531.

Bronfenbrenner, U. (1979). *The Ecology of Human Development: Experiments by Nature and Design*. Cambridge, MA: Harvard University Press.

Lewin, K. (1931). Environmental forces in child behavior and development. In C. Murchison (Ed.), *A Handbook of Child Psychology*. Worcester, MA: Clark University Press.

Lewin, K. (1935). *A Dynamic Theory of Personality*. New York: McGraw-Hill.

Lewin, K. (1938). *The Conceptual Representation and Measurement of Psychological Forces*. Durham, NC: Duke University Press.

Piaget, J. (1954). *The Construction of Reality in the Child*. New York: Basic Books.

2

FROM ECOLOGY OF HUMAN DEVELOPMENT TO DEVELECOLOGY

What we call a field of study is important. The label helps us identify what is to be studied and how. It also may set boundaries, limiting the topic or the methods.

In his writing, Bronfenbrenner used the phrase "the ecology of human development" to refer to his work. The focus was to be human development, and he wanted to examine the environment, or context, in which development occurs. He defined the field this way:

> The **ecology of human development** involves the scientific study of the progressive, mutual accommodation throughout the life course, between an active, growing human being and the changing properties of the immediate settings in which the developing person lives, as this process is affected by relations between these settings, and by the larger contexts in which the settings are embedded.
>
> *(DEFINITION 1, Bronfenbrenner, 1989, p. 188)*

This definition draws attention to crucial aspects of Bronfenbrenner's views, assumptions, and intentions. First, he intends to forward a **scientific**, research-based framework in which the assumptions about reality, the principles, and the definitions of concepts are as clear and concise as possible. In a scientific framework, testable hypotheses can be derived, and appropriate research strategies described. Second, he views humans as **active participants** in the process of development, engaged in continuing **adaptation** to an environment, an environment that includes relationships with other persons. Third, the environment is assumed to be changing, rather than static, and to be adapting to the developing person, so the **accommodations** made by the person and the

environment are **mutual and reciprocal.** Fourth, he conceives the environment as consisting of different **settings,** some of which the person participates
in. Next, the process of mutual accommodation is affected by the relationships
between settings, or parts of the environment. Finally, the process of mutual
accommodation between person and settings is influenced by the larger context—community, society, and culture.

As Bronfenbrenner continued his work, his focus changed and his intent
broadened. In his 1979 book, he hoped to convince researchers to put the
environment into the study of human development, to pay attention to the
context, and offered his framework to help them conceptualize the ecosystems
in which development occurs. As his thinking progressed, he took on the
broader task of explaining the complex role of the ecosystem in development,
and began to describe his work as an "Ecological Systems Theory of Development." As he moved more deeply into the processes of development, his attention turned to examining the role in development of biological change, and the
difficult task of understanding the transactions of genetically driven changes
with changes in the ecosystem. At this turn, he referred to his task as creating a
"Bioecological Theory of Development," which would recognize the equal
partnership of nature and nurture, heredity and environment. As he expanded
his work further to incorporate the importance of attending to the psychological
and social processes involved in the development of the biologically changing
person in a dynamic ecosystem, others were moved to use the "biopsychosocial-
ecological model of development." Bronfenbrenner headed off that prolifera-
tion of prefixes in his own work by referring to his understanding of
development as a "Person-Process-Context Model." This has the advantage of
being easy to remember and encouraging attention to all three components. He
later added "time" to his label to make it a "PPCT" model of development.

In this sequence of labels, we see Bronfenbrenner engaged in two tasks:
defining a field—the ecology of human development—and naming the model
of development he was constructing, as it went through a number of elaborations. At the heart of his work is the desire to meld ecology and development.
In my view, he never quite succeeded in finding the right label for what he was
trying to do. For his model, the term "bioecological" places biological aspects
of development in a privileged position compared to psychological and interpersonal aspects, and thus fails to express the more encompassing integrative
nature of our expanding understanding of human development. Are we to look
only at biology and the ecosystem? The PPCT label for the model works well
enough. For the field of study, "Ecology of Human Development" is useful,
but suggests that human development might be studied without considering
ecology. That is clearly not what Bronfenbrenner believed, and is not the reason
he defined all the concepts within his framework in terms of the developing
person's engagement with the environment. The real power of his framework is
that it *combines a developmental viewpoint with an ecological viewpoint.* Bronfenbrenner

argues for the necessity of applying both perspectives at once, simultaneously, and integrating them into a systemic, comprehensive understanding. But the developmental and ecological viewpoints are usable separately. Development can be and often is considered out of context, or in a very limited context. In fact, that is precisely why Bronfenbrenner developed his conceptualization: to encourage us to think about *development in a context* that is an *ecosystem*. The concept of *ecology* incorporates notions of *systemic relationships*, in which the important elements are related to each other in ways that make changes in one element both productive of and responsive to changes in other elements. Just as development can be considered out of context, however, ecosystems can be analyzed non-developmentally. Ecosystems can be described statically, as if they don't change. How can we describe an approach that is both ecological and developmental, equally, at the same time?

Develecology

The power of Bronfenbrenner's framework lies in truly merging developmental and ecological views. The integration of the two perspectives results in a combined analytic power that far exceeds that of even the sum of the two. In my teaching, I began to use the phrases "ecological developmental framework" and "developmental ecology." Over time, the two sets of principles became so necessary to each other in my thinking that I coined the term *develecology* to refer to the integration of the two sets of principles.

"Develecology" refers to the study of the processes of development within an ecological framework, or the study of development in context. It brings into the general realm of scientific ecology a specialization devoted to the ecology of developmental processes. I believe it is a term usable in other fields as well. My focus, like Bronfenbrenner's, is on human develecology, but I can easily imagine someone else focusing on canine develecology or the develecology of Arctic mammals, for example. Because my interest is in how the study of develecology can be used to improve human conditions, I have come to call myself an "applied human develecologist."

Coined terms require definition, so, to define the term more precisely:

> **Develecology** is the study of the processes of development of organisms and their changing relations with their environments, employing a combination of systemic and longitudinal perspectives that include the mutual and reciprocal transactions of organism and context. The focus of develecological analysis is transactional *change* in both the context and the organism over time.

Develecology fits within a broader framework of the familiar notions of **system**, **ecology**, and **ecosystem**. A *system* is any set of parts or components that work together to make up a functioning whole. _Ecology_ is the study of the relation-ships of living things with their environment and with each other. _Ecosystem_ is a contraction of the phrase "ecological system," meaning a system made up of a set of living organisms and their physical environment and the relations among them. From these notions branch concepts such as bioecology, human ecology, and, now, develecology.

Recent developments in conceptual formulations of development are con-sistent with Bronfenbrenner's framework, and with the notion of develecology. Among these is the work of the late Esther Thelen, which she referred to as a "dynamic systems approach." Thelen's work on early motor development captures the essential integration of transactional effects of biological changes and actions within a dynamic ecosystem (Thelen & Smith, 1994).

The concept of "transaction" in systems thinking attempts to capture the principle that any action by one element of a system affects the other parts, and in turn, reciprocally, actions by any of the other parts will affect the original actor. In this case, when a person acts, or changes, effects will be experienced in other parts of the ecosystem, which will change the ecosystem, in turn affecting the person. A critical aspect of a transaction between any two elements of a system is that _both are changed_ in the course of the transaction. Transactions are what happens between two components in a _living system_ and are always bidirectional.

The central concerns of develecology are to explore what changes in a person and in the environment are important in shaping development. Deve-lecologists hope to learn how the processes of adaptation and accommodation change as a person develops. As we proceed to explore Bronfenbrenner's frame-work, I encourage you to practice keeping both perspectives, developmental and ecological, in mind at each step.

References

Bronfenbrenner, U. (1989). Ecological systems theory. In R. Vasta (Ed.), _Annals of Child Development, Vol. 6, Six Theories of Child Development: Revised Formulations and Current Issues_ (pp. 187–249). London: JAI Press.

Thelen, E. & Smith, L. B. (1994). _A Dynamic Systems Approach to the Development of Cognition and Action._ Cambridge, MA: MIT Press.

3

THE FRAMEWORK

Person and Context: The Challenge of Complexity

Bronfenbrenner's scheme is a system of concepts: *the person* exists in a system of relationships, roles, activities, and settings, all interconnected. *Individual development* takes place as the developing person ages, constructs an understanding of his or her experience, and learns to act effectively within the system in which she or he is participating. Simultaneously, the development of the person *changes the system.* The system changes because as a person develops, his or her actions change, and other people in the system therefore respond differently to the developing person. At the same time, the *settings* the person participates in are interrelated with each other and with other settings. As well, the settings are part of the culture in which the whole system of settings and the roles, relationships, and activities within them are embedded. We will examine one by one the parts of the system, their interrelationships, and their impacts on development as we work to understand the processes of the whole.

The task we are undertaking is not a simple or easy one. It is a great challenge to understand the interrelatedness of a complex living system such as the social system we live in. It requires prodigious expansion of our mental structures to conceptualize relationships that constantly shift, and that act reciprocally on each other. The challenge is doubled because some aspects of relationships are part of the immediate experience of the person, while other aspects are more abstract, removed from the direct experience of the person. To then place the constantly changing, developing person within that dynamic system further enlarges the challenge.

Bronfenbrenner attempted to help us conceptualize the human ecosystem with an analogy to a set of nested Russian dolls, with the person in the middle encased in a series of hollow dolls, representing levels of the system, each larger than the next (1979, p. 3). Another analogy sometimes offered is an onion, with a series of layers that can be peeled away. Both analogies are misleading.

In the set of dolls, each level is independent, though parallel—simply larger or smaller in scale. In develecology, the layers or levels are *not* simply bigger or smaller. Each is of a different *kind.* The *microsystem* is one level, but the next level, the *mesosystem*, is not merely a larger microsystem; it is the *relationship* among the settings of the smaller "nearer" level, or microsystems. The two levels are not just different in size, but otherwise identical. They are in fact different, the larger consisting of the *relationships* among the smaller, and thus *incorporating* the smaller, not existing independently of it, as the nesting dolls do. We will continue to elaborate our understanding of this complexity, but it will be necessary to overcome the implications of Bronfenbrenner's own insufficient nesting doll and onion analogies. We will use Figure 3.1 to organize the framework, building it part by part as we proceed.

Bronfenbrenner presents his framework in the terms of science, stating his *definitions*, explaining his *assumptions or propositions*, and constructing formal, testable *hypotheses* about the way things work or are related in development in the environment. I'm going to present Bronfenbrenner's hypotheses as if they are true, but remind you here and elsewhere that Bronfenbrenner was trying to encourage research, and to create a scientific approach to the study of development in context. A future challenge for you is to see what evidence you can

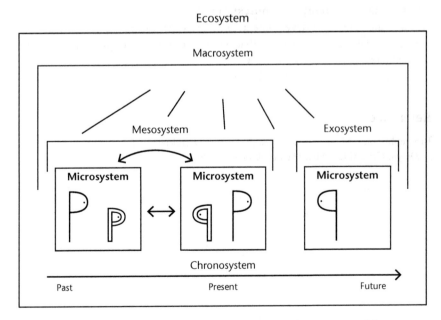

FIGURE 3.1   The structure of Bronfenbrenner's Ecological Systems Model

find for the validity of his hypotheses. Are they supported by research? Are they evident in your own experience? Are they consistent with the conclusions of others who think about development? Bronfenbrenner hoped that we would test the validity of his hypotheses, refine them, and add to them as we construct a more sophisticated understanding of development in context.

The primary purpose of Bronfenbrenner's scheme is to lead us to understand the development of the person in the ecosystem in which the person participates. Bronfenbrenner couches his framework in scientific terms, and emphasizes the importance of designing ecologically sound research. Nevertheless, his lifelong purpose was to design, promote, and evaluate policies and programs that would improve society and support development of children and families. Because many students of human development come to the topic motivated to help people, to teach, and/or in other ways to make the world a better place, I focus in this book on applying Bronfenbrenner's framework, and develecology more generally, to the task of facilitating development.

We attempt to facilitate development in many ways. We teach, we raise children, we counsel, we create social services, we give money to worthy causes, we pass laws and write policies, among others. The essence of facilitating development is to create environments, relationships, or activities that support and enhance the person's understanding of the world and ability to function in it. How do we know our efforts promote development and wellbeing of the people who are the targets of our efforts? Bronfenbrenner argues that to design effective strategies and to assess their effectiveness, we must understand the processes of **development in context**. In the following exposition, we will examine the context of development, and how variations in the person's experience in it shape development so that we might answer the question: How do we facilitate a person's development?

We will turn now to look at the person.

Reference

Bronfenbrenner, U. (1979). *The Ecology of Human Development: Experiments by Nature and Design*. Cambridge, MA: Harvard University Press.

4

THE PERSON AND DEVELOPMENT

Bronfenbrenner sees human beings as active participants in the world. In his view, we are always interacting with our environment, and these interactions are reciprocal: the world interacts with us. Analysis of the nature of the inter-actions or transactions we have with the systems in which we participate is key to explaining development. Understanding how we develop within the eco-system is the central issue in Bronfenbrenner's work.

We are always learning about the world through *active experience* in it. The human mind is designed to make sense of experience. Intelligence is a characteristic of humans that enables us to construct understanding of our world, our experi-ences, and ourselves. As we develop we gain understanding, which we apply to our ongoing experience, gradually building up knowledge and understanding, and gradually refining our abilities to function effectively in our world. People are always engaged in the fundamental process of *adapting to the ecosystem* we are in. Intelligence can be considered the abilities to understand the experience we have and to use that understanding to adapt more effectively to the environment. The processes of development include biological changes in our ability to act in the world, cognitive changes in our ability to understand the world, and psychological changes in our ability to behave effectively in ways that are appropriate to the situ-ations we encounter and the relationships we share with others.

Bronfenbrenner's view is fundamentally constructivist, similar to the approaches of Piaget, Montessori, Erikson, Vygotsky, and other theorists of human development. In all these theories, it is the person who is actively con-structing an individual mind, based on the biological potentials humans have evolved over time. In constructivist theories, then, to understand a person's development is to explore the *gradual change in understanding* constructed by the person through experience in a world.

To Bronfenbrenner, it is important to keep in mind that the individual is constructing a unique and personal understanding, a conception that may be shared with many others, but which fundamentally is the individual's own. The person's view is based primarily on the specific and unique experiences the person has had over time in a specific and unique environment or ecosystem. If we want to understand the person and the person's unique development, we have to try to understand the particular ecosystem the person has experienced, over time. And that ecosystem must be examined from the person's own viewpoint, or perspective. Bronfenbrenner regularly returns to the notion that there is not an external objectively true or "real" environment in which the person is participating: there is only the environment the person perceives and interprets. What is developmentally important is the ecosystem as the person perceives and experiences it. So, to understand development we must attempt to *see the ecosystem from the perspective of the developing person in whom we are interested.*[1]

What we are trying to explain, in Bronfenbrenner's view, is the essence of development, the understanding of the world the person is constructing, along with the skills the person is acquiring, skills that will enable the person to act effectively within the world. Bronfenbrenner's emphasis on understanding and skills developed in transaction with a specific environment is incorporated in his definition of development:

Human development is the process through which the growing person acquires a more extended, differentiated, and valid conception of the ecological environment, and becomes motivated and able to engage in activities that reveal the properties of, sustain, or restructure that environment at levels of similar or greater complexity in form and content.

(DEFINITION 7, Bronfenbrenner, 1979, p. 27)

Let's break up this definition into its component parts. Figure 4.1 represents the developing person.

The Growing Person

The developing person changes over time. Changes are inherent in human growth. The person changes biologically, and the biological changes themselves are in part shaped by the nature of the person's participation in the ecosystem. Examples of transactions in which the *ecosystem alters biological change* would include these, among many others:

1   If the ecosystem does not afford food adequate for good nutrition, the person's biological growth reflects the inadequate nutrition.

FIGURE 4.1   The developing person

2   If the ecosystem encourages practice of particular motor skills, the person will develop better motor skills than would be the case if the person participated in an environment without such opportunities.

Similarly, the biological changes taking place change the nature of the person's participation in the ecosystem. Examples of transactions in this direction of the transaction include:

1   Learning to walk makes it possible for the child to explore the ecosystem more broadly and to reach places that were unavailable to the infant.
2   Puberty typically makes the person a potential sexual partner in the eyes of other members of the ecosystem. So, the transactions the person has with those other people will change because their view or understanding of the developing person changes, and the other people will behave differently. They will gradually assign a new role to the developing person, not necessarily on the basis of the developing person's new *behavior*, but because of *their perception* of the person's biological changes.
3   Pregnancy changes one's role in the ecosystem but also may change one's ability to move quickly or to carry out tasks as one has previously.
4   Slowing of reflexes or perceptual changes in the later years may alter how one can participate in the ecosystem.

Thus, the biological characteristics of the person, characteristics that change regularly through the life span, help *determine* the person's participation in the ecosystem, and in turn, those biological changes *are influenced by* the nature of the ecosystem and of a person's participation in it.
Biological characteristics are significant in the experience of the person in the ecosystem in other ways as well. *People differ* biologically. That is one of the

wonderful features of humanity. We differ by sex, skin color, facial characteristics, body type, distribution of hair and its characteristics, shape of our faces, feet, hands, and so on and so on. Our brains also differ. We have genetically based differences in our propensity to develop a variety of skills. We have different temperaments, different physiological responses to a variety of stimuli, and different characteristic emotional tones and reactions to experience and events.

Each of us is a unique variation on the human paradigm. Our experience of the environment reflects the influence of many of these characteristics. Some of us may be attracted to a setting that exposes us to music and provides opportunities for musical exploration, while others of us might find such a setting less interesting. Some may enjoy physical challenge, and seek out opportunities to run, climb, ride, or jump.

At the same time, the subtle and not-so-subtle differences among us often have *meaning to others* in the ecosystem. Differences from others in the setting may have meaning in a setting, and thus shape the transactions we have in it and the nature of our participation and experience in the system. For example, if a person's sex is a basis for exclusion from some activities in a setting, then being male or female will determine one's participation and experience in the setting, as it does in all cultures. In a setting in which some skin colors are valued above others or where dark skin makes one subject to exclusion or differential treatment, then the biology of skin color will shape experience. Less dramatically, perhaps, in a family of quiet, reflective people, a child with a high energy level and desire for physical activity may have different experience and develop a different view of self and of others than the same child would in a family of high-energy active athletes.

Thus, biologically based variations affect our participation in our ecosystems in several ways. Our biology may lead different people to engage in different activities, different roles, or different sorts of relations in a particular setting. In the longer view, development is shaped by the accumulated effects of those variations in experience and variations in the ecosystem itself, as some settings may be open or closed to our participation.

The variety of transactions between biology and experience/environment are summarized in Figure 4.2.

Conception of the Ecological Environment (View of the World)

Knowledge and understanding are the result of the perceptual, cognitive, and psychological processes humans employ. Psychological processes underlie participation in the world. People perceive, remember, process information, distort, think, practice skills, seek experience, explore, try things out, etc. In most developmental theories, these psychological processes of engagement in the world are essential mechanisms of change and development. We call these processes "*proximal*," because they are directly in the experience of the person.

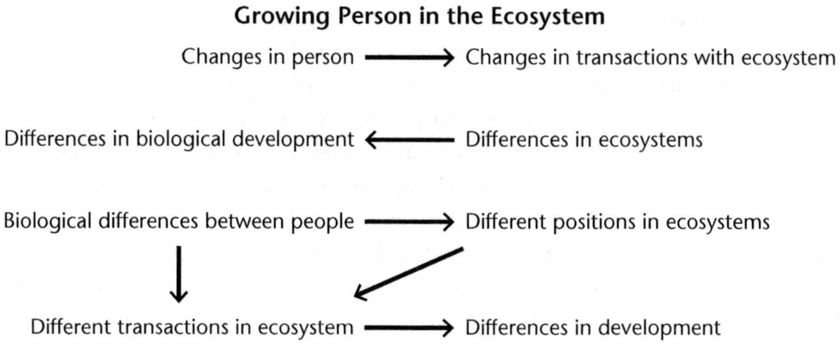

Growing Person in the Ecosystem

Changes in person ⟶ Changes in transactions with ecosystem

Differences in biological development ⟵ Differences in ecosystems

Biological differences between people ⟶ Different positions in ecosystems

Different transactions in ecosystem ⟶ Differences in development

FIGURE 4.2 Transactions between biology and environment

Bronfenbrenner assumes all these psychological processes are ongoing, thus change along with biological development, and that they are affected by experience in the ecosystem, by participation in the ecosystem. Describing or explaining developmental changes in essential psychological processes is not a focus in his framework, but understanding them is necessary for analyzing changes in participation in the world. So, students of development must still study and comprehend the many theories and domains of development that focus on those processes.

As the biologically changing person experiences the ecosystem in increasingly sophisticated ways, there are more experiences, and more to understand. The understanding constructed covers more of the ecosystem, becoming more extended, and has more details, becoming increasingly differentiated, or having more parts.

To Bronfenbrenner, what is important about the knowledge and understanding constructed by the person is whether they are complex and valid—valid in the context of the specific experiences the person has had. Does the knowledge we construct help us understand the experience we have? Are we seeing our surroundings clearly, and understanding how our world functions? Are we able to anticipate or predict what will happen? Can we adapt or cope with changes more effectively? As we develop more valid understanding, we also may become more able, or skilled, at exploring and changing the world, able to participate in our environment more effectively, safely, and comfortably. In Bronfenbrenner's view and in his definition of development, it is the practical understanding and skills we develop that are most important. The development he describes is always in part an adaptation to the ecosystem the person is in.

When Bronfenbrenner refers to an ecosystem, or some component of an ecosystem, as "facilitating development" or "enhancing development," he is referring to promoting human development as defined in his Definition 7. Development is facilitated either when the person's view of the world becomes more valid, extended, and/or differentiated, or when the person becomes more motivated and able to act in ways that are more effective in managing or living in the environment. It is important to keep his definition of development constantly in mind as we learn to use the develecological framework.

We are used to saying that people *learn from experience*. Experience comes from or is the result of transactions we have with people and with settings—the ecosystem. People employ their mental processes to make sense out of their transactions and the ecosystem in which they occur. Making sense of our experience produces a view or conceptual understanding of the experience, the ecosystem, and ourselves. As we develop, our view of the ecosystem becomes *more extended*—it covers or includes more experiences and more of the ecosystem. Our view becomes *more differentiated*—we see the ecosystem in more detail, with more parts, and more differences among the parts. Our understanding also becomes *more valid*—our understanding becomes more consistent with the ecosystem we exist in, and therefore more useful to us in the process of adapting to the ecosystem we experience.

Development also consists, in Bronfenbrenner's definition, of becoming *more motivated* and *more able* to investigate, explore, manipulate, take care of, and change the ecosystem we experience. His definition of development thus takes into account that people are curious and that our skills and potentials change as we grow. Our brains and our mental processes mature and respond to the experience we have, making it possible for our understanding to become more complex. Our bodies change to permit greater mobility, more dexterity, and more strength to use in exploring and maintaining the environment we are in. So we become more skilled, more able. And why would we become *more motivated* to engage in activities like those he includes in his definition? Curiosity is a type of motivation. Perhaps humans want to understand and be comfortable in their environments, so the activities that fit the definition represent our ways of *adapting to* the ecosystem and *adapting it* so we understand and fit in it better. Perhaps we want to be competent, and being able to do something motivates us to do more, and thus become more competent.

Notice, too, what Bronfenbrenner's definition of development *does not include*. It is not about IQ, test scores, grades, or vocabulary, or speed of processing, or memory capacity. It is specifically about our understanding of our eco-

system and our competence in transacting with the environment. Thus, Bronfenbrenner's definition of development is about our adaptation to the ecosystem that is shaping our development in it. Defining development in this way, Bronfenbrenner works to make his framework as internally consistent as possible. An ecological view of development is about developing in, understanding, adapting to, and functioning within the ecosystem.

Finally, in Bronfenbrenner's scheme, the developing person can be any person at *any point in the life span*. As long as the person is adapting to the ecosystem, working to develop a more valid understanding and improved skills, the person is developing. In many of the definitions and hypotheses that follow, Bronfenbrenner uses the phrase "developing person" to refer to the person whose development we are focusing on, the object of our attention.

Adaptation | Ecosystem

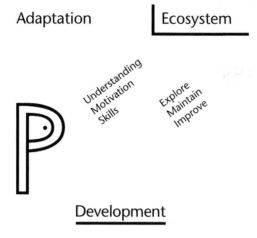

Development

FIGURE 4.3   Components of development

Remember: In Bronfenbrenner's view of development: Development happens within a person who is assumed to be growing and changing biologically. Development is the result of transactions with the ecosystem. Development is changing the person's transactions with the ecosystem, and the ecosystem is also changing. Development consists of three elements:

1   The person's understanding of the ecosystem becomes increasingly differentiated, extended, and valid.
2   The person becomes *more skilled and thus able* to explore, maintain, and transform the ecosystem.
3   The person becomes *more motivated* to explore, maintain, and transform the ecosystem. As the person develops, his or her ability to adapt to and function in the ecosystem improves.

Figure 4.3 summarizes Bronfenbrenner's concept of development as adaptation to an ecosystem.

Now let's move on to consider what people *do* in the ecosystem.

Note

1   For discussion of this phenomenological view and its importance in Bronfenbrenner's Definitions, see Bronfenbrenner, 1979, pp. 22–34.

Reference

Bronfenbrenner, U. (1979). *The Ecology of Human Development: Experiments by Nature and Design*. Cambridge, MA: Harvard University Press.

5

ACTIVITIES

People act. Action is inherent in being alive, as a human being. Activity is intrinsic to our encounters with the world we live in, our environment. Our activities, like our understanding, tend to become more complex as we develop. In a constructivist view, complex activities evolve or are constructed from the exercise and coordination of less complex ones. In Bronfenbrenner's words "activity is at once the source, the process, and the outcome of development" (1979, p. 289).

How is activity related to development? In the previous section, we examined Bronfenbrenner's definition of human development. If development is the process of acquiring a more extended, differentiated, and valid understanding of the eco-system, what does that process involve? How do we acquire that understanding? We come to understand the environment because we experience it, because we observe it, because we act on it, and interact with it. Our activities in the environment lead to understanding that environment. Beyond that, as we develop, the activities we engage in to explore the environment, to maintain it, and to change it become more complex skills. And as we repeat and practice those activities, we become more skilled in understanding, exploring, and transacting with the environment. Engaging in activity in the environment (where else could one engage in activity?) is a central component of the process of developing.

What kinds of activity are important in development? Connecting to the definition of development, we might propose that any activity would be of interest if it contributes to the process of one of the components of development as Bronfenbrenner defines it. We should distinguish simple *actions* from *activities*. An *action* might be anything one does, such as breathe, twiddle one's thumbs, cough, or throw a stone into a pond. Dictionary definitions of *action* focus on single movements, acts, or deeds. An *activity* refers to something larger, or more important, a specified *pursuit*, in dictionary terms. An activity might be an action or a set of actions that one is learning to do, or that represents a new skill or way of transacting with the world, or that has the potential to change the person or the environment or both. Bronfenbrenner proposes to distinguish between *molecular*, or simple, actions and *molar*, or larger, meaningful activities. In physics, *molar* refers to a body of matter as a whole, rather than its atomic or molecular properties or subparts. Bronfenbrenner uses *molar* to indicate we are interested not in the minutiae of actions, but on larger activities or behaviors the person focuses on or pays attention to and that are important to the person, and potentially to the process of development.

> A **molar activity** is an ongoing behavior possessing a momentum of its own and perceived as having meaning or intent by the participants in the setting.
>
> *(DEFINITION 12, Bronfenbrenner, 1979, p. 45)*

This definition suggests that a molar activity has three main characteristics: it is *ongoing*, has *momentum* of its own, and is perceived to have *meaning or intent*. *Ongoing* means that the activity occurs over a period of time. If an activity occurs over time, or periodically, it is likely to be related to development, and perhaps also has potential to change. *Momentum* is the tendency of something to continue or proceed. People tend to continue an important activity to its conclusion. If a molar activity is interrupted, the person may feel frustrated, and may be motivated to return to the activity so it can be completed. *Meaning or intent* refers to the reason the person is engaging in the activity. Why is the person doing the activity, why is it important enough to expend energy on? Our activities usually have a purpose or goal, especially if they are activities that have "intent—the desire to do what one is doing either for its own sake or as a means to an end" (Bronfenbrenner, 1979, p. 46). From a *developmental perspective*, the activities of interest would be those that have the potential to become incorporated with other activities into more complex activities. From a *person perspective*, we might focus on the activities that are important to the person, the ones the individual attends to and doesn't want interrupted, will return to if interrupted, frets about, or expends significant effort on. From an *ecological perspective*, important activities would be the ones most likely to reveal the properties of the environment, or sustain or modify it. Is it helpful to focus on the activities that combine all three of these characteristics?

What counts as molar? While it might be satisfying to make a list of which activities are molar and which are not, it is not easy to do that. Whether an activity is molar or not depends on the person, the person's intent, and the person's development so far. Activities change over time, as they become coordinated and integrated into larger activities. For an infant, learning to stand without holding on might be the most complex activity in the repertoire, the one with most *meaning* and *momentum*. Infants expend great amounts of energy and time, intensely focused as they work hard to learn to stand. Certainly, learning to stand is a molar activity at that time. As the infant masters that activity, the activity may become less molar, as it is incorporated into the more complex activity of walking. As walking becomes the focus and standing is mastered, and no longer requires concentration and effort, standing ceases to be molar. Walking becomes the new molar activity, and standing simply a subordinate part of the new activity. The developing person moves on to focus on incorporating walking into running, and running into soccer dribbling, and soccer dribbling into playing soccer, and playing soccer into winning a state championship, and so on (and on), perhaps to becoming a revered soccer coach. Each of these becomes in turn a molar activity incorporating all the previous molar, now molecular, components. As the person moves from lesser to greater complexity, the activities that were once molar become just actions, no longer molar. The new, more complex behavior becomes the molar activity that has meaning and intent, and which the person is motivated to continue.

Sometimes the developing person's *intent* also determines whether an action becomes an activity. Breathing, for example, is an action that is reflexive throughout our lives, and not molar, even though it is ongoing and has momentum and we intend to keep on doing it. But it is automatic, and we spend almost no time thinking about it. Breathing can, however, become a molar activity if we change our intent and the meaning we assign to it. Examples of this might occur when we decide to learn the specific pattern of breathing associated with yoga or meditation, or if we decide to learn the pattern of circular breathing musicians use to maintain a note without interruption, or if we want to learn to breathe effectively while we swim using the crawl or freestyle stroke. Each of these ways of breathing requires attention, effort, and practice, making them new molar activities, no longer simply reflex action. Even so, the new intent depends on the use of the new skill in the more complex molar activity of yoga, playing an instrument, or swimming.

The point that a particular activity that is molar at one time but not later, or when our intent changes, is important to keep in mind. It means that what counts as molar is not fixed, but changes with time and circumstance, with development, with intent, and perhaps environment. Molarity is relative to coordination of the activity with other activities. This is the reason we can't create definitive lists of molar and non-molar activities. We will see that other elements in the ecosystem also change over time, as their relationships to development and to the other elements change. We change, and our ecosystems change, and both are central to explaining development.

The process of constructing more and more complex and integrated activities is a fundamentally important way to look at development. It is an example of what Piaget calls the progressive process of coordinating knowledge. Bronfenbrenner directs us to look at how the ecosystem we participate in encourages the development of specific molar activities and how those activities become more complex. Does the ecosystem support the developing person's construction of more complex activities, and more differentiated and valid understanding of the ecosystem?

Degree of Development

That activities change and may become incorporated into increasingly complex activities leads to a related idea. Bronfenbrenner suggests that we might use the activities a person engages in as a measure of maturity, or developmental status. Specifically, he proposes:

> The **developmental status** of the individual is reflected in the substantive variety and structural complexity of the molar activities which she initiates and maintains in the absence of instigation or direction by others.
>
> *(PROPOSITION B, Bronfenbrenner, 1979, p. 55)*

How many different things can you do, and how complex are they? What activities do you actually engage in when you get to do what you want to do, on your own? This approach to assessing developmental status is quite different from the more traditional indices. This is not about chronological age, or biological maturity. It is not about IQ or any paper-and-pencil or other kind of test. Importantly, it is not about what a person *can* do, but rather about what a person *does* do, when the person is in charge of his or her own behavior. In this, Bronfenbrenner is being consistent with his definition of human development. Developmental status is relative to the environment one is in, and has to be assessed within the person's ecosystem. It is a measure of how well the person has adapted to the environment, learned what is possible to do in it, and is able and motivated to engage in those activities. Of course, actually creating a measure that would allow us to rank people on the basis of this index of maturity would be a difficult task. Nevertheless, the proposition encourages us to think about what other measures we use actually do reflect. His point is that assessing relative maturity in an ecological framework requires we focus on how a person engages in the ecosystem.

Note that Proposition B states only that developmental status is *reflected in* the variety and complexity of molar activities a person engages in. It does not say that this is the *only* measure of developmental status or maturity. The definition of human development implies other ways to measure development. We could propose that maturity is reflected in the extent, differentiated-ness, and validity of the person's understanding of the ecosystem. Another part of the definition suggests maturity might be reflected in the person's ability and motivation to engage in activities that reveal, maintain, or rearrange the ecosystem. Or these could be combined. The immediate challenge here would be constructing an assessment of these characteristics of the person, a challenge shared with Proposition B. But all three possibilities are significantly different than other measures of maturity because they are directly connected to the person's adaptation to the ecosystem.

Bronfenbrenner provides an example of how we might think about the challenge to assess degrees of development, or changes in development, in his hypothesis about research on the impact of early childhood education on development. He proposes that if we really want to measure the developmental effects of programs like Head Start, we should not look for changes in IQ or achievement tests, but should look for changes in molar activities and relations with others (Hypothesis 20, Bronfenbrenner, 1979, p. 201).

Let us examine a couple of examples of how differences in the complexity of activities might reflect different levels of development. Consider the toddler learning to walk. At that time in life, walking is a molar activity, one to which the child devotes great energy, and the practice of which keeps the toddler (and parents) awake in the middle of the night. Much later, having mastered walking, the person might learn about exercise, nutrition, and other good health practices. As an adult, the person may incorporate walking into the much larger and complex molar activity of maintaining a healthy lifestyle.

As another example, consider two 20-year-olds in college, roommates. What do they do when they have free time? One surfs the channels on television, watching whatever comes up. When asked later what she did through the afternoon, she reports she watched TV. What did she watch? Shows, nothing important. The other, given free time, goes to the gym, writes e-mail home, organizes his closet, reads a book. If he watches TV, he seeks out programs from which he can learn about the news of the day, and incorporates that into his political science essay, interpreting the news, etc. In other words, for one, the couch potato, television fills the available time. For the other, the one Bronfenbrenner would describe as more highly developed, television is one of a number of important activities, but important for its connectibility to other activities and responsibilities.

Activities and Other People

Because activities are so important to us, and we are social animals, the activities that others engage in are of interest to us. Because we are attracted to the activities of other people, their activities are important to our development. The more varied and complex the activities we observe people around us do and that they engage in with us, the more developed we will become (Hypothesis 1, Bronfenbrenner 1979, p. 55).

The important activities as we develop are going to be the ones that we engage in with other people, in joint activity. And we are going to learn more, and practice those activities more, in relationships that we enjoy. As we engage in activities over time, in relationships we enjoy, the activities are likely to become more complex, and thus we become more developed. This emphasis implies that if our environment *does not* include people who engage in complex and varied activities, or if those people do not engage us in their activities, we will not develop as well as we otherwise might.

Bronfenbrenner and Morris (1998, pp. 996ff.) apply these principles in the following way to describe the role of "proximal" or immediate experiences in development:

1   For development to occur, the person must engage in an activity.
2   To be effective, the activity must take place "on a fairly regular basis, over an extended period of time." For example, this means that in the case of young children, a weekend of doing things with Mom or Dad does not do the job, nor do activities that are often interrupted.
3   Why not? One reason is that, to be developmentally effective, activities must continue long enough to become "increasingly more complex." Mere repetition does not work.
4   Developmentally effective proximal processes are not unidirectional; there must be influence in both directions. In the case of interpersonal inter-action, this means that initiatives do not come from one side only; there must be some degree of reciprocity in the exchange.
5   Proximal processes are not limited to interactions with people; they also can involve interaction with objects and symbols. In the latter circum-stance, for reciprocal interaction to occur, the objects and symbols in the immediate environment must be of a kind that invites attention, explora-tion, manipulation, elaboration, and imagination.

Why focus on activities? Because activities are what we develop. It is our activ-ities that are our successes and our accomplishments. And it is our activities that represent deficient development. Success in school is the result of appropriate molar activities. Failure in school is the result of activities that are not congruent with the expectations of the school setting. Parenting is a molar activity. How we parent is crucial for the development of the next generation. For most of us earning a living is a molar activity. Income may be proportional to the complexity of the activities we engage in, and perhaps to their scarcity in the ecosystem. Maintaining a drug addiction is a complex molar activity. Leadership in one's community is a molar activity. In other words, explaining how we develop complex activities that are important to us and to those around us is essential to understanding our development in our ecological context. Remember that Bron-fenbrenner's definition of development includes becoming "motivated and able to *engage in activities* that reveal the properties of, sustain, or restructure that environ-ment *at levels of similar or greater complexity* in form and content."

ongoing
momentum
intent

Activities

FIGURE 5.1 Molar activities

Often, when we are responsible for the development of other people, we choose or direct the activities *they* engage in. Develecologically, it is important that we consider whether those activities have the potential to become more complex over time, and whether they will be sustained over time. Can and will the activities be continued in the absence of our direction? Do the activities contribute to the person's *development*—to understanding of the world and ability to function in it?

A *developmentally facilitating environment* will include many opportunities for people to engage in molar activities. It will allow those activities to become more varied and more complex. It will include opportunities to be in the presence of people who engage in a variety of complex activities, to observe, participate in, and learn those activities, and eventually to carry them out on one's own, and to choose to engage in them.

Remember: Molar activities have three important characteristics: they are ongoing, they have momentum, and they have meaning to us (see Figure 5.1). Activities are important in development because they are the means by which we learn about our environment and develop skills. As we develop, our activities become more complex and make us more competent in our ecosystem. Our development is facilitated by having other people around us who engage in complex activities and who engage us in those activities.

References

Bronfenbrenner, U. (1979). *The Ecology of Human Development: Experiments by Nature and Design.* Cambridge, MA: Harvard University Press.

Bronfenbrenner, U. & Morris, P. A. (1998). The ecology of developmental processes. In R. Lerner (Series Ed.) & W. Damon (Vol. Ed.), *Handbook of Child Psychology: Vol. 1. Theory* (5th ed., pp. 993–1028). New York: Wiley.

6

DYADS AND RELATIONS

Developing people engage in activities. We may engage in activities alone, and activities done alone may be important, especially as an index of our level of development. In the preceding section, Bronfenbrenner highlights the importance to development of *activities we engage in with others*. Activities in the context of significant relationships are the ones we are likely to focus on and elaborate. Relationships with others are central in most explanations of development. The people in our lives and our relations with them are crucial components of our ecosystems. We are social animals, and transactions with other people are central to our experience from birth on. In many ways, our development is manifested in *changes* in our relations with other people. Dyads and relations are the interpersonal structures created by our awareness of other people in our environment.

Relations are the transactions that occur by the participation of two or more people with each other.

> A **relation** obtains[1] whenever one person in a setting pays attention to or participates in the activities of another.
>
> *(DEFINITION 13, Bronfenbrenner 1979, p. 56)*

The smallest number of people who can relate to each other is two, so Bronfenbrenner focuses on the dyad.

> A **dyad** is formed whenever two persons pay attention to or participate in one another's activities.
>
> *(Bronfenbrenner, 1979, p. 56)*

Dyad refers to the two people as depicted in Figure 6.1. The *relation* is what happens between them.

A person may participate in several dyads. If there are two people in a setting, there is one dyad. If there are three people, there would be three dyads. Four people can create six dyads, five people ten dyads, and so forth. How many dyads are possible when your family convenes? Or your class? How many could there be in your workplace?

Of course, we could talk about larger, more complex groups. If there are three people in a setting, there are three dyads, but there is also one triad. Four people can make up six dyads, and they can also form four unique triads and a tetrad. We focus on dyads for a couple of reasons. First, the dyad is the simplest relation, so understanding the transactions that go on in a dyad would be the foundation for attempting to understand more complex relations. Second, it is likely that a majority of significant transactions among people occur in dyads. Do we attend to more than one person at a time? How often? How important to our development are simultaneous transactions with two or more others? Third, as a practical matter, it is difficult enough to comprehend and describe the transactions that occur in dyads. As each additional person is added, the transactions become exponentially more difficult to describe. These reasons do not lead to the suggestion that analysis of relations larger than dyads is not important. Indeed, such analysis may be crucial in understanding family systems, group functioning, and social psychology, among other endeavors. But we will focus on dyads as the basic unit.

Just as every person is unique, every dyad is unique. As well, the relation in the dyad may be seen or understood differently by each person. Each has a perspective from which to view the relation, and their perceptions of it may be very different. They may be similar, but it is not necessary that they will see the relation the same way, or agree on how to describe it. Going beyond or outside

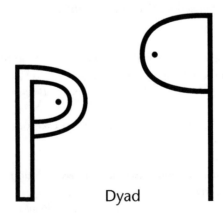

FIGURE 6.1 Dyad

Bronfenbrenner's work for a moment, a relation is also abstract, like a system. In fact, we can refer to a **two-person system**, meaning the relation. The relation is what happens *between* the two people. The relation is *different from* the two people. The relation is not the *sum* of the two people. A relation is seen in the transactions that occur that involve two individuals, so the relation is a *process*, or a set of processes. The relation is constructed by the actions of the two parties. Neither party alone can create a relation, though either may instigate it. Additionally, the relation can be altered by either person. Whenever one person changes his or her behavior in a relation, the relation is changed, and it is likely the other person will modify his or her behavior to continue the relation. The transactional nature of dyads is assumed by Bronfenbrenner when he proposes:

> If one member of a dyad undergoes developmental change, the other is also likely to do so.
>
> *(PROPOSITION C, Bronfenbrenner, 1979, p. 65)*

In this proposition, Bronfenbrenner assumes that the ongoing transactions with another person are an important part of the experience of the developing person. Any developmental change—a change in the person's view of the world or skills and motivation for dealing with the environment—will alter the person's actions in the dyad. That alteration will affect the transaction. The other person will experience the changed transaction and attempt to adapt to it. The process of adapting to the changed transaction will lead to developmental change on the part of the other. Why? Because human *relationships are transactional*. Both parties are trying to make the relation comfortable and productive. They constantly *re-calibrate* the relationship, or adjust their behavior to *accommodate* any new action or emotion of the other. The relation *adapts* to changes in either party. Bronfenbrenner's Proposition C refers to a kind of ongoing calibration and re-calibration of the relationship in the dyad. As two people try to maintain an interesting, predictable and comfortable relationship, each will respond to any change by trying to adapt, and to create a new homeostasis, or comfortable, predictable, and stable state. If one of them develops, in any of the ways Bronfenbrenner defines development, the second person may attempt to maintain a stable relationship, at first by resisting change. If that disrupts the harmony of the relation, the second may then adapt by changing, and the re-calibrating attempt may invoke change in the second person—a change in view, or skill, or motivation that is compatible with the change in the first person.

Thus, in develecology, development of any member may change the transactions in the relations others have with that person, and as each other person responds to the changes in those transactions, *their* development may be stimulated, and the entire system may be changed in some way. This principle is fundamental to family systems theory and other systems frameworks. Change in any one element may provoke change in other elements and in the functioning of the whole system.

Types of Dyads

Bronfenbrenner describes several *types of dyad* (1979, pp. 56–59). Dyads take three basic forms, different in function:

An **OBSERVATIONAL DYAD** occurs when one member is paying close and sustained attention to the activity of the other, who, in turn, at least acknowledges the interest being shown.

A **JOINT ACTIVITY DYAD** is one in which the two participants perceive themselves as doing something together.

A **PRIMARY DYAD** is one that continues to exist phenomenologically for both participants even when they are not together.

An *observational dyad* is created whenever one person pays attention to the actions of another, and the other is aware of being observed. A *joint activity dyad* is formed when two people engage in a common activity. A *primary dyad* forms when two people see themselves as *relating to* each other, and think about each other even when they are not together. Note that the definition of a primary dyad does not *require* that the two people be apart for the dyad to be a primary one. It is a primary dyad even when, and perhaps *particularly* when, the two people are together, engaged in joint activities. But, unlike the other two forms of dyads, the people in the dyad are likely to think about each other when they are not together. Participation in the primary dyad is likely to influence a person's behavior even when the other person in the primary dyad is not present. This is what Bronfenbrenner means by "phenomenologically." The other person continues to be part of one's experience and one's ecosystem, even when not physically present. In a primary dyad, both people *continue* to think about each other, and to be influenced by those thoughts, even when they are not together. The dyad does not *become* primary only when the two people are not together.

All your family dyads and your dyads with good friends are likely to be primary dyads. They're *primary* because they are important. They're so important that you *continue to think about each other* even if you're not together. They're primary dyads when you're together, and they *continue to be primary dyads* even when you're apart.

They *don't become* primary dyads when you part; they *already were* primary dyads.

In his Hypotheses 2 and 3 (1979, p. 59), Bronfenbrenner suggests that observational dyads tend to turn into joint activity dyads, and joint activity dyads tend to become primary dyads. Why? Because people tend to be attracted to activities and to people who engage in them. Then, if people engage in joint activities over time, they may begin to think about the other person and the activities. If the activities are enjoyable, they may want to engage in them again, and thus may seek to initiate contact and activity.

The types of dyads described refer to important characteristics of the relation between the two members of the dyad. The types are not mutually exclusive, however. Members of a primary dyad are likely to engage in joint activities with each other, turning some primary dyads into dyads that are both joint activity and primary. We refer to a particular dyad by using the label that designates the most complex function or "highest" level of the relation (1979, p. 58).

Also important in our later analyses will be the *transcontextual dyad*, one that exists across two or more settings. Transcontextual dyads are those that occur across settings, regardless of whether the relation is observational, joint activity or primary. Thus a particular dyad may be a transcontextual joint activity dyad. If you participate in a dyad with the same person at home and in another setting as well, it is a transcontextual dyad. Bronfenbrenner also defines a *developmental dyad*, which we will discuss later (Section 7).

Hypotheses 2 and 3 emphasize the potential for dyads to change, or develop. Changes in dyads over time represent one way ecosystems change as people grow. The nature of the relations we participate in and the activities we engage in with other people are *essential elements of the social system* in which we develop.

Transaction

Let me elaborate on the notion of *transaction* in relationships. People act, producing *actions*. Others may respond, producing a *reaction*. When we consider the combination of the action with the reaction, we are studying an *interaction*, or what goes on between the two people. The prefix *inter-* means *between, within, mutual,* or *reciprocal*. Many actions evoke specific and/or predictable reactions from the other person, and the nature of the reaction may determine the further response or reaction of the original actor. Thus we may see the process going on between the two people, the interaction, as a unit, a set of coupled or conjoined actions and reactions. Bronfenbrenner often refers to the "ping-pong game" that goes on between parent and child, referring to the reciprocal behaviors, or interactions, so important in development.

In what way is a *transaction* different? One meaning of the prefix *trans-* refers to *change* or *transfer*. A transaction is a particular type of interaction, one in which the two parties engage in actions and reactions, but the *result of the interaction* is a more or less permanent *change in one or both partie*s. As an analogy, think about what happens when you enter a store and ask about a particular item. That's an action. The salesperson's response is a reaction, so you are engaged in an interaction. If the establishment doesn't have what you want, or you can't afford it, the interaction remains an interaction, and you leave unchanged, aside from knowing something more about the store and its offerings. The salesperson is also unchanged. If in the next establishment, however, you find what you want and buy it, you engage in a *transaction*. You leave with the item, and the salesperson retains your money, so there has been an *exchange* and both of you are changed. If an interaction, either immediately or over time, results in a lasting change in either or both parties, then it can be called a transaction.

In develecology, it is change, or development, that is of greatest interest, and so it is most important to examine the *transactions*, the activities and interactions occurring in relationships that *lead to change*. We have to be able to describe the dyads and relations a person participates in, the activities the dyad engages in, and how those dyads change over time, to begin to understand the person's development.

A *developmentally facilitating ecosystem* will include the opportunity to form multiple dyads with different people. It will allow the person to engage in joint activity dyads, and to participate in primary dyads. Thinking back to the previous section on activities, we can combine the concepts to suggest that an ecosystem that promotes development will provide dyads that engage in and teach increasingly complex activities. As we proceed through discussion of each element in Bronfenbrenner's framework, we will pause and reach back to bring the previous sections forward, constructing bit by bit a more complex and layered system that integrates all the previous concepts with the current one.

Remember: A dyad is two people who are aware of each other. Bronfenbrenner describes three types of dyads, that differ according to what the people in them are doing: Observational, Joint Activity, and Primary. Later we will learn about a fourth type of dyad, a Developmental dyad. A relation is what is going on between the two people in a dyad (see Figure 6.2). Relations are of many

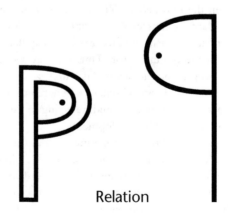

FIGURE 6.2   Dyad and relation

different kinds, depending on the specifics of the three major characteristics of relations: Affect, Power, and Reciprocity. We turn next to examine those characteristics.

Note

1 Here, Bronfenbrenner uses "obtains" to mean *exists*.

Reference

Bronfenbrenner, U. (1979). *The Ecology of Human Development: Experiments by Nature and Design*. Cambridge, MA: Harvard University Press.

7
IMPORTANT CHARACTERISTICS OF RELATIONS

Now, what characteristics of relations are important? Bronfenbrenner proposes that of all the potential characteristics of dyadic relations, three properties are likely to be most helpful in understanding the role of relations in development: affect, power, and reciprocity.

Affect refers to the feelings people experience. How two people feel about and act toward each other creates the emotional tone of a relationship. Is it generally positive, warm, loving, and affectionate, or at the other end of the spectrum, is it hateful, negative, cold, unloving, or disrespectful? The affect of the relationship may be neutral, or it may be ambivalent, if people aren't sure how they feel. Affect in a relationship may be inconsistent, or might be asymmetrical, if two people feel differently about each other. It may be obvious that relations that are on the positive end of the affect continuum are more attractive and appealing to us, while those at the negative end we attempt to avoid, end, or change.

Relationships differ in affect, with some being more positive than others, and the affect in some being stronger than in others. The affect in a relationship may *change* over time, becoming more negative or more positive. We are likely to prefer to spend time in dyads that have positive affect and disengage from dyads with more negative affect. Similarly, as the affect in a dyad changes, our interest in participating in the dyad is likely to change accordingly.

Power refers to both the relative strength of each person in the relationship, and to their influence on each other. To what degree can each change the activities the dyad engages in? How much ability does each person have to control or direct the dyad and its activities? Here, too, there is a dimension, or continuum, from relationships in which one person has all or most of the power, and the other has none, to relations where the two participants are equals, where there is a *balance of power*. Bronfenbrenner assumes that adults have more power than children, that teachers have more power than their students, for example. And the balance of power can change. As we develop, and gain more skill, we may acquire more ability to control an interaction or a situation, and we may be granted more permission to exercise control. Over time, a particular relationship may evolve from being very unbalanced to being balanced, with equal power residing in each party. As my colleague Armin Grams was fond of saying, "As parents, our goal is to raise our children so that when they are adults they can stand beside us, as equals."

Reciprocity refers to the mutual sharing or transactional character of the activities and interactions that take place in the relation. Do the two parties take turns initiating activities? Do they each respond to the other? Do they alternate responsibilities? Do the people modify their actions to accommodate each other, so their activities become more mutually coordinated? At one end of the continuum of possible relationships, there is complete reciprocity, mutuality, and sharing, and at the other end, no reciprocity, a relation in which one party initiates actions, but does not respond to the initiatives of the other, or a relation in which *neither* shares anything with the other. Are people more likely to prefer dyads with a high degree of reciprocity, or low?

Reciprocity may be seen when people take turns in conversation, share information with each other, or alternate roles. In good relationships, for example, people may do favors for each other or help each other. They may be equally interested in how the other feels, or what the other thinks, and move toward understanding each other well. Reciprocity may mean they each listen to the other as much as they talk about their own views, or that they take care of each other when one is ill.

These three properties of relationships are relatively independent of each other. What possible combinations of the three might exist? How would various combinations be experienced? What other characteristics could one look at? How else can relations be described, and how do they differ? If you could write scripts for different kinds of relations, how might they read, for example, for a relationship that had *no* reciprocity? What would the dialog be in a relationship with very unbalanced power, where one member had far more power than the other? It may be easy and more familiar to imagine a conversation between two people in a relationship with very strong negative affect, or very positive affect.

In Bronfenbrenner's view, all relationships can be described using these three dimensions (see Figure 7.1). He distilled these three from the extensive literature on relationships, attempting to capture the few characteristics that would apply to all relationships and that would be most clearly related to differences in the activities engaged in by different dyads and most clearly related to the roles of the dyad in development. Differences in where particular relations fall on these dimensions are helpful to understanding why *people develop differently depending on what kinds of relationships they engage in.*

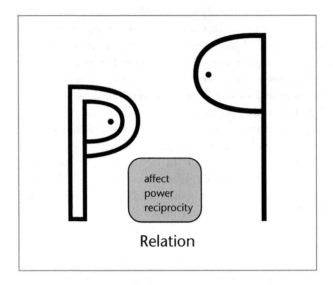

FIGURE 7.1 Relation and its characteristics

Dyads, Relations, Activities, and Development

Now that we have looked at the types of dyads and the characteristics of relations, we can ask how dyads and relations affect development in the ecosystem. Does it matter what different types of dyads we have or what the characteristics of our relationships are? Bronfenbrenner offers Hypothesis 4 to suggest that it does.

> The developmental impact of a dyad increases as a direct function of the level of reciprocity, mutuality of positive feeling, and a gradual shift of balance of power in favor of the developing person.
>
> *(HYPOTHESIS 4, 1979, p. 59)*

In this hypothesis, Bronfenbrenner asserts that relationships in which the *affect is positive*, the *reciprocity high*, and the *power* becoming more *equally balanced* are the relationships that have the most positive influence on us. "Direct function" here means that developmental impact rises and falls in concert with the levels of the three characteristics that follow in the hypothesis. Developmental impact rises as the level of reciprocity in the relation increases. Developmental impact falls if the mutuality of positive feeling declines. And developmental impact is better if the power gradually shifts toward the developing person, and is worse if the power shifts away from the developing person. It might be worth adding that dyads that are consistent with Hypothesis 4 might be the most enjoyable.

In this and many other hypotheses, Bronfenbrenner specifies a "developing person." Of course, all of the people in an ecosystem are likely to be developing.

When we refer to the "developing person," we mean the person whose development we are trying to explain. As we will see later, it is necessary to choose a person to focus on, because the ecosystem is defined and labeled from that person's perspective.

Hypothesis 4 specifies the characteristics of the relation in a dyad that will impact development. Does it matter what the dyad is *doing*? Remember that activities are fundamental to development. Bronfenbrenner provides hypotheses that focus on this question. Observational learning is a source of experience and information that occurs sometimes in the context of an observational dyad. In Hypothesis 5 (1979, pp. 59–60), he suggests that learning by observing might be more likely and more effective if the people in a dyad are engaged in a joint activity. Observational learning is the focus of Hypothesis 5, though the hypothesis may also apply to directed or intentional learning. Observational learning is important because often we assume that children and other developing people are influenced by their environment "by osmosis," by absorbing or picking up cues, understanding, attitudes, and knowledge simply by being exposed to the environment, without direct tuition, or teaching.

Hypothesis 5 also illustrates a point made in the discussion of dyads earlier—that a dyad may be of more than one type. Hypothesis 5 suggests that a dyad might be an observational dyad and a joint activity dyad at the same time. Could such a dyad also be a primary dyad? Perhaps, but it might be unwieldy and unnecessary in most cases to use all three labels together. If it is primary, it may typically involve observation and joint activity—though there may be circumstances when that is not true. In Hypothesis 6 (1979, p. 60), Bronfenbrenner switches from talking about observational and joint activity dyads to considering the activities going on in the situation. The hypothesis asserts that learning by observation and engaging in joint activities will both be greater if they take place in a primary dyad characterized by positive affect.

Let me return to the point just made about primary dyads. While it is *possible* for a dyad to involve two or even all three types—observational, joint activity, and primary—it is not *necessary* that a primary dyad include either observation or joint activity. A parent and child would be expected to form a primary dyad. Yet even though each may think of the other often when they are not together, it might be that during a prolonged separation, the dyad might engage in no observation of each other and no joint activities. Hypothesis 6 also suggests that a primary dyad does not necessarily involve positive affect. Indeed, it may be that people who dislike each other, or fear each other, might think of each other often, and in so doing influence each other's development.

In another hypothesis about learning and development in dyads, Bronfenbrenner considers the ideal combination of a dyad, characteristics of the relation, and nature of the activities that might have the greatest developmental potential. He hypothesizes that development will be facilitated by participating in joint or reciprocal activity that becomes gradually more complex, in a primary dyad, with positive affect, and when the balance of power shifts toward the developing person (Hypothesis 7, 1979, p. 60).

This last hypothesis presents the ideal characteristics of a relationship Bronfenbrenner defines as a fourth type of dyad, a *developmental dyad*. This is an important addition because in analyzing the relationships that are important to the developing person, we will be seeking the dyads that have the capacity to foster development, and trying to understand why some relationships do not foster development. A **Developmental Dyad** is one in which there is reciprocity and mutual positive affect, the joint activities become progressively more complex, and the balance of power gradually shifts in favor of the developing person (1979, p. 60). The concept of Developmental Dyad is different from the other basic types of dyad because it refers to *changes* in the dyadic relationship over time.

Multiple Dyads

It may be obvious, but it is still important to say that people in dyads affect each other. We refer to the effects people have on each other as **first order effects**. First order effects are the direct impact people in dyads have on each other because they are interacting, and trying to maintain a relationship. Environments may contain more than one dyad, and the dyads are not independent of each other. A person may be participating in several overlapping dyads, and the relation a person experiences in one dyad is likely to affect the relation a person has in another dyad. Thus one dyad may affect other dyads each person may be participating in with other people. These indirect effects of participation in one dyad on participation in another dyad are recognized by Bronfenbrenner in his Proposition E (1979, p. 68). These indirect effects are referred to as **second order effects**. Second order effects are the ways dyads affect each other, while first order effects are the ways people affect each other. As we attempt to understand the effects of environments on development, we will have to try to account for both the first order effects and the second order effects, if the environment includes more than two people.

To illustrate the effects of dyads on each other, it might be useful to think about someone who has a primary dyad with a good friend, perhaps a roommate. If the person then establishes another primary dyad, perhaps with a new friend or a romantic partner, several second order effects are possible. One is that the person will have less time to spend with the original friend, and the characteristics of their relation may change. A second possibility is that the original friend and the new person may not like each other, causing stress for the person in both dyads. Analyzing second order effects is essential in understanding any relation, such as a couple, or system of relations, such as a family.

Bronfenbrenner considers the important impact of dyads on each other as they affect their ability to serve as developmental dyads (Hypothesis 8, 1979,

p. 77). He suggests the ability of a dyad to support development is greater if other dyads the parties are in share positive affect with the original dyad and are supportive of the activities the potentially developmental dyad engage in.

An instructive example to illustrate this hypothesis is the Mother–Father–Child triad. The triad includes three dyads: Mother–Father, Father–Child, and Mother–Child. Hypothesis 8 suggests that each of the dyads affects the other two, and thus, that each person has an effect on the dyadic relationship of the other two. The mother–child dyad impacts the parental dyad, and may interfere with or support the development of the father–child dyad. Similarly, the father–child dyad affects the parental dyad, and may shape the mother–child dyad. Specific possibilities are many, but include the possibility that the reciprocity and positive affect of the mother–child dyad might cause jealousy and tension (negative affect) in the parental dyad, and that conflict or hostility in the father–child dyad might encourage greater positive affect and granting of more power to the child in the mother–child dyad. This sort of mutual influence among dyads is fundamental to the study of family systems and the emotional dynamics within them.

It may be helpful to create a summary of the important characteristics of relations, and how they are related to development. Remember that it is necessary to specify whether affect is positive or negative or neutral. Just saying the affect in a relation is *"strong"* leaves the reader wondering whether the people love or hate each other. Similarly, a description of a relation must indicate whether reciprocity is high, medium, or low, and whether the power is equal, or balanced, or very unbalanced, and if so, in whose favor.

It may be helpful to *distinguish between* the *power a person has*, or that is attributed to the person, and the *power the person actually exercises* in the relation. The latter, the power a person actually employs in transactions, is what shapes the relation in the dyad. For example, we may understand that a parent *possesses* considerably more power than a child. The parent, however, may *actually exert* very little power in transactions with the child or may exert a moderate amount of power. The *power actually used is what the child perceives*, and is what the child responds to.

When relationships *change*, one or more of these characteristics is likely to change. This means that when we describe a relationship that is changing, it is necessary to describe the change in each of its characteristics. Is the affect more negative or more positive? Is there more or less reciprocity between the two people? Has the balance of power shifted toward one person, or become more balanced? Describing these changes then provides the basis for assessing whether the changes make the relation more or less likely to support the development of the developing person.

In addition to describing the three characteristics of a relation, we can use the other hypotheses we have studied to suggest analyzing the activities the people in the relation share. Changes in the number and complexity of the joint activities the people engage in and changes in the settings they occupy are important indicators of how the relation may be affecting the development of the people in it. As we continue, we will also see many other hypotheses that will address other elements of the ecosystem that may shape the characteristics of the relations a person participates in.

A *developmentally facilitating ecosystem* will provide opportunities to form relations with mutual positive affect and a high degree of reciprocity, and in which the balance of power is moving toward a state of balance. It will also include multiple relations in which each person is supportive of the developing person's participation in the other dyads, so the dyads are mutually supportive. Environments that allow the dyad to engage in more complex joint activities will facilitate development. Events or alterations in the ecosystem that result in any of these changes will support development. Conversely, when relations have negative or neutral affect, a low degree of reciprocity, and the developing person continues to have less power than others, development will be hindered.

Remember. The relation in every dyad can be described using the three essential characteristics. *Affect* can range from very *highly positive* to very *highly negative*, with *neutral* in between. You cannot describe the affect as "very high" without specifying whether it is highly positive or highly negative. *Power* can range from *greatly unbalanced* in favor of one person to *greatly unbalanced* in favor of *the other*, with *balanced equally* in the middle. *Reciprocity* can range from *very high* to *very low*, with *moderate* in the middle.

Reference

Bronfenbrenner, U. (1979). *The Ecology of Human Development: Experiments by Nature and Design.* Cambridge, MA: Harvard University Press.

8

ROLES

To this point, we've seen that the environment includes people engaging in activities and participating in dyadic relations. Another feature of environments is that the people in social systems have different functions or play different roles. What is a role?

A role is a set of activities and relations expected of a person occupying a particular position in society, and of others in relation to that person.
(DEFINITION 14, Bronfenbrenner, 1979, p. 85)

Roles are a major component of culture. Each culture contains typical roles and the expectations for how to carry them out. Infant, child, teenager, young adult, student, parent, husband, wife, teacher, doctor—the list of roles is endless. *Roles incorporate both activities and relations*, the two elements considered in the preceding sections. A role comprises *expected activities*: parents are expected to guide their children, husbands nurture and partner their wives, teachers provide a curriculum, doctors doctor, etc. Roles also are defined by activities that are *not* permitted, or not appropriate for the role. Teachers do not take bribes to grant A grades to students. Students do not threaten teachers; parents don't ignore their children—at least not good parents, parents who are carrying out the role appropriately. Psychotherapists don't have sexual relations with their patients, or talk about their clients' problems at parties. These expectations for activities also then shape the expected relationships the person in a role engages in with other people. Reciprocally, the expectations embodied in a role also shape *how other people behave* in relationship to the person in the role.

As participants in a society, we learn the roles we encounter, along with the expected behaviors and activities appropriate to each. We see the roles that are common to our experience in books, stories, media, theater, entertainment of all sorts. Children rehearse important roles in their dramatic play, exploring how roles relate to each other, and what the expectations for each role are and how to play them, and how roles relate to each other. We learn to recognize when the role is being played appropriately, and when someone is violating the expectations for the role. Thus, when we are put in a role, or in the position of relating to someone in a particular role, we know what to do. In Hypothesis 9 (1979, p. 92), Bronfenbrenner predicts that when we are put into a familiar role, we are likely to try to fulfill its expectations, and other people are likely to try to behave appropriately toward us.

Roles are more or less clearly defined or delineated in a culture, and may differ in how flexible they are and how much variation there is in how different people play them.

Bronfenbrenner proposes in Hypothesis 10 (1979, p. 92) that when roles are clearly defined and the defined expectations are broadly agreed upon in a culture, people will be more likely to both play the role in the expected way, and relate to the person in the role appropriately. His Hypothesis 11 (1979, p. 92) suggests that the tendency to play roles in the expected ways is even greater if the role is one that is defined to have power in a social system, and other people are not likely to resist if the occupier of the role exercises that power. When great power is accorded (part of) a role, people are likely to submit to it, and become passive (HYPOTHESIS 11, 1979, p. 92).

Roles are often paired, or complementary to each other, and the relations in the dyads defined jointly for each role. Examples of paired roles are parent and child, teacher and student, wife and husband. Roles also exist in larger sets. Such a set would be student, teacher, principal, aide, parent, and coach, in a school setting. Another set would include patient, nurse, LPN, doctor, resident, and intern, in a medical establishment. If everyone in a set is filling his or her role as expected, then others are more likely to fill theirs as expected as well (Hypothesis 12, 1979, p. 94).

Expectations for specific roles may vary, so how they are defined, and how others play their complementary roles, will lead to different performances of the role. For one example, Bronfenbrenner draws on research that manipulates game and play expectations in group situations. When a social setting, such as a summer camp, emphasizes competition and games where people win or lose, campers are likely to become more competitive in other activities as well. Conversely, if the camp emphasizes collaboration and team-building, campers become more cooperative with each other in general (Sherif et al., 1961). These findings support his Hypothesis 13 (1979, p. 101), that people tend to meet the expectations that are defined for a particular situation

The general principle underlying this hypothesis is that people tend to adapt to and follow the expectations for a role that are expressed by the group of which they are a part. What other examples of this principle can you think of?

How might this hypothesis apply to children's behavior in classrooms with different expectations, or our behavior in families where people are expected to be helpful and supportive, in one case, or sarcastic and punitive in another?

Social ecosystems include a variety of roles, which are part of the structure and function of the system. Ecosystems differ in which roles are present, and in how those roles are defined and performed. As we experience an ecosystem and adapt to it and learn the roles, our understanding of the social environment and our ability to function in it are constructed. Bronfenbrenner predicts that development is promoted by experiences of playing a variety of roles as well as by engaging in activities with people who themselves play a number of different roles (Hypothesis 14, 1979, p. 104). Why would this be? Perhaps because roles are important structures in the social ecosystem. The more experience a person has playing and interacting with different roles, the better one will understand the environment and be able to participate in it. These, of course, are components of his definition of development.

Roles are defined by the activities engaged in by a person in the role, but are also defined by the kinds of *relationships* that are expected or appropriate, as depicted in Figure 8.1. Children respect and follow the guidance of their parents, parents nurture their children, police officers protect citizens, teachers guide students. If it seems that roles and activities and relationships are all connected to each other, and confounded with each other, that's right. Roles have prescriptive properties: If you are put into or assume a role, your behavior and your relationships are prescribed. When children engage in dramatic play, they

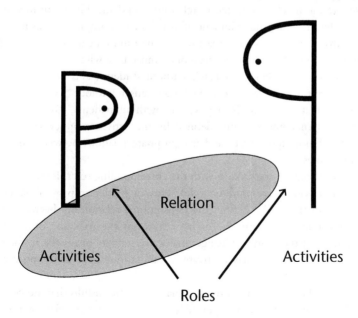

FIGURE 8.1   Roles incorporate expectations for activities and relations

are rehearsing and sorting out their understanding of these prescriptions. If you're playing the "daddy," you have to do certain things, and relate to others in particular ways.

The Importance of Roles

Our understanding of the roles we fill guides our behavior. Our understanding of how others should fill their roles guides our expectations of them and our reactions to and behaviors toward them. We praise others who carry out their roles appropriately or well—who fit our expectations. We say they serve as exemplars or models for how the role is to be played. When someone's behavior violates our expectations for a role, we call them bad mothers or incorrigible or unmanageable children, poor students, abusive teachers, or corrupt officials. Some roles are prescribed in law. Failure to carry out the role results in sanctions for what we call "misconduct." We encourage people to be "good role models" for others, and blame undesirable behavior on exposure to "poor role models."

The conflicts we have with others are often *conflicts over the definitions or understanding of our roles*: "husbands shouldn't treat wives that way." "You should be more thoughtful of my feelings. You forgot my birthday!" Roles are important shapers of what happens in relationships and settings. Differences in role expectations create conflicts in relationships and may make it more difficult to understand and adapt to a role or to a setting.

Roles are intimately connected to relations, and defined by them in a second way. Very few roles are independent of other roles. Many *roles are defined transactionally*, that is, by their counterpart roles. One cannot be a parent unless there is or has been a child. In most cultures, one cannot be a wife without a husband, and vice versa. A teacher can't teach without students, and one cannot be a student without a teacher. One can't be an abuser without a victim, a judge without criminals or plaintiffs, a physician without patients. Our most significant roles often come in pairs, defined by the activities prescribed for both sides, and defining appropriate and inappropriate relations between the occupants of the roles.

Roles are *learned* in transaction with the corresponding roles. Roles are *played* in transaction with corresponding roles. How a particular pair of people, or dyad, carry out their roles defines the transactional relationship between them. If one person alters the way she or he carries out the role, the other can be expected to resist the change. Changes may cause anxiety or distress in the other member of the dyad, and may motivate re-calibration of the affect, power, and reciprocity in the relation.

One of our basic human efforts is to maintain relationships that are comfortable and familiar. Thus, if one person changes how he/she plays a role, the other is likely to change how she/he plays the corresponding role to make the relationship comfortable, and to make it effective or adaptive in the social system in which they are playing out the roles. This process underlies and is a major tenet of *transactional conceptions of relationships*. One *cannot* change the other person; one *can* change one's own behavior. Changing one's own behavior in turn will alter the relation one has with the other person, and the other may alter his/her behavior in response. Thus, AlAnon urges people who live with alcoholics to consider how their own behavior *supports* the alcoholic's drinking, to stop trying to change the alcoholic, and to *alter their own behavior* so as to reduce the impact on them of the alcoholic's addiction. Similarly, marriage therapists encourage clients to stop blaming the partner and to alter their own behavior to change the relationship in ways they want. In other words, if you are in a transactional role that is dissatisfying, it is more effective to try first to change the way you play *your* role than to try to get the other person to change how he or she plays his or her role.

Roles are one type of conceptual building block for social systems. Examining what the roles are and how roles are organized is part of conceptualizing social systems. Social institutions define and incorporate particular roles and their definitions. A nuclear family has parents and children. An extended family has uncles, aunts, and grandparents as well. Many important roles are *kinship* relationships, that is, defined by biological or legal connection. Other roles are *functional* roles: A large business has a president or chief executive officer, treasurer, vice president, managers, workers, accountants, advertising executives, and so on, endlessly. A religion has, for example, a pope, cardinals, bishops, priests, acolytes, parishioners, etc. Roles in social organizations often are arranged hierarchically. This implies that the roles exist in their own *system* of roles.

Roles may change or evolve over time. The particular roles included and how they are defined and prescribed is a component of culture or subculture. "European cultures" define roles in families differently than do "Asian cultures." Anthropologists study the variations in roles across cultures. They and sociologists study the variations in roles and the changes in roles across societies and across time. What influences those role changes and variations? Social psychologists study (among other things) how roles are defined and how they influence behavior. They study how changes in the way a role is played affect the perceptions and behavior of those who relate to the role. When cultures evolve, roles may change, or the way they are played may change, or both. For example, the roles referred to by "gay" or "woman" have undergone considerable change in our culture in recent years.

A person may occupy several roles. How *congruent* are the roles? Do different roles carry *different expectations*? How do we cope with differences among the roles we play? A person may be a wife and mother at the same time. How *compatible* are the roles? Are they in conflict? We speak of role *conflict*, role *overload*, or *competing* role *demands*. How do we understand and cope with those? When we come to focus on the mesosystem, we will see that people are likely to play different roles in different settings. A person is likely to be both a teacher in school and a parent at home, and may be an adult child in her own parent's home.

Summary

So, in Bronfenbrenner's framework, activities and relationships are embedded in roles. A role is defined by the activities expected of the person in the role and the way the person is expected to relate to others. Roles relate to each other. People play roles and how they play those roles contributes to how other roles are played. Changes in how one person carries out a role may produce changes in how others carry out their roles. Within a culture, specific roles are defined similarly. Differences in how roles are defined are one of the manifestations or components of differences between cultures. In the process of developing, we learn to play roles we are put into and we learn to relate appropriately to the roles others fill. How well we learn the activities prescribed for our roles is a determinant of our success in carrying out the roles. Our understanding of the roles is part of our view of the ecosystem. Our ability to fill a variety of roles is part of our skill in functioning in our ecosystem. The roles available to us contribute to defining our place or status in the ecosystem.

An *ecosystem is more developmentally facilitating* if it contains a variety of roles that children and others can practice filling, and a variety of roles they can interact with. It is not essential that roles be clearly defined or strongly agreed on; those are differences among ecosystems, but they don't limit the *variety* of roles available to developing people. It may or may not be important that the roles a person fills be congruent or compatible with each other. Conflict between roles one occupies may be stressful, and that *might* hinder development. On the other hand, learning to resolve or accommodate such conflicts might represent enhanced development, as the person adapts to the ecosystem and acquires more skill in managing it.

Remember: A role includes:

1   specific activities and how these should be carried out;
2   the way the person in the role relates to other people; and
3   how other people are expected to relate to the person in the role.

References

Bronfenbrenner, U. (1979). *The Ecology of Human Development: Experiments by Nature and Design.* Cambridge, MA: Harvard University Press.
Sherif, M. et al. (1961). *Intergroup Conflict and Cooperation: The Robbers Cave Experiment.* Norman: University of Oklahoma Book Exchange.

9

SETTINGS

So far, we have introduced Bronfenbrenner and his ideas about the person, development, and the activities, relations, and roles the person engages in. Now let's turn to Bronfenbrenner's ideas about understanding the environment. *Where* do activities, relations, and roles occur? What *locations* are important in the large world where we reside and behave? How are we to make sense of the incredibly complex diverse world that surrounds us? Bronfenbrenner proposes that the feature of the environment that is most useful to distinguish is the **setting**. A setting *is a place with definable physical features*. In a setting, people can have face-to-face interactions (1979, p. 22). As we will see later, the essential feature of a setting is that it can contain a system that involves people and their activities. A setting that doesn't contain people is probably not developmentally important.

> Different kinds of settings give rise to distinctive patterns of role, activity, and relation for persons who become participants in these settings.
>
> *(PROPOSITION F)*

How big can a setting be? Is a corner of a room where a conversation is going on a setting? Is a classroom? A university? A neighborhood? South Africa? There is no hard and fast rule about how big a setting can be. But since the importance of settings lies in the system of roles, relationships, and activities that occur in them, a practical limit is whether we can describe the system that is contained in the setting. Thus, to describe all the activities, roles, and relations that occur in a university would be a much bigger, and perhaps impossible, task than defining the system in which a person can engage within a specific classroom or in a room in a residence hall.

Since the purpose of develecological analysis is to understand the processes of development, the focus of describing a setting would be the participation of the developing person. It may also depend on the level of abstraction at which we are working. Later, when we begin to look at the relationships among different settings, how the settings are related to each other—the mesosystem and exosystem—we will return to this discussion. When we do, we may propose, for example, that the university might be a setting because we are looking at how it relates to a person's other settings, such as home and work, or previous settings, such as high school. For that purpose, it may be useful to consider the university as a single setting. If, however, our task is to understand the person's participation within the university as it affects development, then it may be useful to consider the university as containing a variety of settings, or sub-settings, and to look at how they relate to each other: the connections between classroom and residence hall or athletic field, for example. In practice, the determination of what is a setting depends upon our purposes and whether we can define and describe the system of relations and activities that occur in it.

Each particular setting has characteristics that determine what can take place within it. Many settings are designed specifically to shape and support activities in particular ways. Baseball and polo and swimming, for example, require different settings. A house may be divided into rooms, each equipped differently, designed for different functions. Sleeping may be uncomfortable in a kitchen, taking a shower difficult in a living room. The design of spaces to *shape behavior* in specific ways is fundamental to architecture and interior design. By the selection and arrangement of furniture, equipment, and other materials, settings are made conducive to relaxation, work, exercise, preparing meals, learning, studying, watching a movie, performing music, and so forth.

The world we live in is made up of many settings. In develecology, awareness of the settings the person passes through and participates in, over time, is essential to explaining development. Additionally, the *impact of the person on the setting* is important in understanding the ecosystem. Again, consider that Bronfenbrenner's definition of development includes engaging in activities that reveal the properties of, sustain, or restructure the environment. We explore settings, we maintain them, and we alter settings to make them fit our desires.

> The developmental potential of a setting is enhanced to the extent that the physical and social environment found in the setting enables and motivates the developing person to engage in progressively more complex molar activities, patterns of reciprocal interaction, and primary dyadic relationships with others in that setting.
>
> *(HYPOTHESIS 19)*

The setting is not, by itself, especially important in understanding development. Specific features of a setting shape or limit the activities that can go on in the setting, but development is the result of the engagement in the activities, the dyads and relationships, and the roles that occur within the setting. Bronfenbrenner formalizes this point in Hypothesis 19 (1979, p. 163) by predicting that a setting will better support development if people in it can engage in activities that become more complex, relations that are high in reciprocity, and primary dyads. This becomes important in develecological analysis because we are likely to have higher expectations for some kinds of settings than for others, reflecting their size, beauty, reputation, or expense. For example, people are likely to assume a small, rundown cabin in need of repair is a less favorable place to grow up than an expensive modern home in an attractive suburb. But Bronfenbrenner is clear that it is not the appearance of the home, or its size, or its cost that determine development in it, but the activities, roles, and relationships that occur within it (Proposition H, 1979, p. 183). If people in two settings have different outcomes developmentally, the differences will reflect differences in the roles, relations, and activities people participate in within those settings. We'll explore such differences in more detail.

As we proceed in exploring Bronfenbrenner's work, we will examine the important features or elements within settings, how they affect the developing person, and ways to change settings so they have more positive effects. A setting that facilitates development allows and encourages molar activities that can become more complex, provides roles the developing person can fill and interact with, and affords relationships that can become primary or developmental dyads. Ecosystems that facilitate development contain a variety of settings that are conducive to activities, roles, and relations that support development in the ways just described.

One central reason settings are important elements of the ecosystem is that we tend to focus on settings when we think about adaptation. When a person first participates in a setting, she or he is trying to understand the setting and what goes on in it, and is trying to learn what activities, relations, and roles are available and expected. If the person continues to participate in the setting, she or he normally will try to fit in it, to become comfortable in it. The process of understanding a new setting and learning what is going on in it takes effort, and may be stressful. It may make a person anxious at first. As the person develops a clearer understanding of the setting and becomes more skilled in it, it becomes less stressful and perhaps even pleasant. As this happens, the person is more able to engage in the activities, relations, and roles available in the setting. The person is likely to become more productive, learn, and otherwise benefit from participating in the setting. If a person cannot understand or adapt to the setting, it remains stressful, and the person's behavior may be inappropriate. The person may "adapt" to the setting by escaping it, or avoiding it, if possible.

An *ecosystem is developmentally facilitating* when it provides settings that allow people to engage in increasingly complex activities, relations that support development, and roles that help them learn more about their ecosystem and develop skills to operate effectively within it.

Settings are Places Where People Can Interact

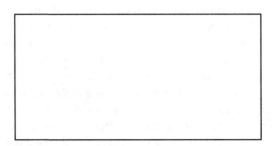

Setting

FIGURE 9.1   A setting

Remember: Settings are places with physical features. Settings are not people, or friends, or family life, high school football, or other activities. People and activities may be *in* settings, but they are not the settings. We must be sure to specify the physical place when referring to a setting.

In the graphic model we are constructing, we will begin with settings, as in Figure 9.1, and then place people and their roles, relations, and activities in the settings.

Reference

Bronfenbrenner, U. (1979). *The Ecology of Human Development: Experiments by Nature and Design.* Cambridge, MA: Harvard University Press.

10

ECOLOGICAL TRANSITIONS

In develecology, change is assumed, and Bronfenbrenner focuses on several types of change or *transition* a developing person may undergo.

> An **ecological transition** occurs whenever a person's position in the ecological environment is altered as the result of a change in role, setting, or both.
>
> *(DEFINITION 6, 1979, p. 26)*

Transitions are a major focus in Bronfenbrenner's framework, as in any explanation of development. We go through many transitions of many different sorts as we develop. Every ecological transition involves a change in role or a change in setting, or both. Changes in role may come about because a person has grown. Becoming a toddler, for example, is a change in role within the family or child care program. Reaching the age of entering school adds the role of student to a child. Some changes in roles happen because other people change their expectations of a person or their relationship with the person. A teenager hired to watch other children takes on the role of babysitter. When chosen, a person may become a boyfriend, a new role. Changes in roles may also mean losses of roles. Losing a job or retiring take a person out of the role of employee.

Changes in setting also take different forms. A person may enter a new setting, as when entering college. One may lose a setting, or stop participating in it. As we saw in the preceding section, settings provide distinct patterns of roles, activities, and relationships. So, gaining or losing a setting in one's life may mean a change in the roles one fills, the activities one can engage in, and/ or one's relationships. And the changes in activities and relationships that are involved in gaining or losing roles or settings may have implications for a person's development.

Not all transitions are *ecological* transitions. To be of particular interest in develecology, a transition must reflect change in role or setting. A forty-third birthday may be a transition, but it most likely does not mean a change in role or setting. One's eighteenth birthday, however, may mean a change in role. Can you think of other transitions that would *not* include changes in role or setting?

Ecological transitions are important in develecology for several reasons. Bronfenbrenner proposes that "every ecological transition is both a consequence and an instigator of developmental processes" (1979, p. 27). So when we consider an ecological transition, either a change in role or a change in setting, or both, we have to think about *what happened that led to* the transition, as well as *what happened because of* the transition. Is Bronfenbrenner right that ecological transitions *happen because* some developmental process has occurred? And does each ecological transition *instigate or lead to* some developmental process?

Ecological transitions are also important in development because *change often causes stress*, even when the change is considered good or desirable. Ecological transitions require learning and adaptation to the new role or setting. Ecological transitions may provide a test of the development that has taken place in previous settings or roles. How could a transition *test* development? By providing a challenge or an opportunity to apply understanding or skills that have been constructed prior to the transition. (We'll examine this idea later in relation to Hypothesis 48 in Section 16.)

Developmental Changes as Ecological Transitions

In human development we often think in terms of stages. Stages represent periods of time during which the person exhibits some particular stable characteristics—and the characteristic of a stage may be change, as when puberty is occurring. But stages have to be different from each other, and the transitions between stages are when interesting things happen. Each stage of human development is introduced by changes in the person that may alter the individual's role in the ecosystem. Two examples may illustrate this:

1   Between infancy and toddlerhood, mobility and language change drastically. Both developments change the child's role in the family, and the activities the child can engage in, as well as how the child relates to others, and reciprocally, how those others relate to the child.
2   Puberty introduces adolescence and renders the individual capable of reproduction. One's role in the social system changes, others react to the change, transactions with others are different because the person and others view the person differently and respond differently; expectations change.

Many of the individual transitions a person experiences are ecological transitions. The names we use for stages, in fact, imply different roles.

Social transitions often involve ecological transitions: entering school is a change in setting as well as the addition of the role of student. Retirement is a change of role from worker to retired person, and typically a change in setting, in that the retiree leaves the workplace. Leaving home for college, or leaving college for work are ecological transitions, as both roles and settings change. Marriage is an ecological transition because the person assumes the role of spouse and typically changes setting to establish the marital household.

Transitions and their characteristics are important in understanding development because ecological transitions affect the ecosystem and one's place in it. Analyses of the characteristics of changes and the subsequent changes in the person's transactions are central to develecology. What ecological transitions are made? *Can* the transitions be made? Does the new role or setting mean the ecosystem is richer and more varied? Hypothesis 14 (Section 8) suggests that if few roles are available to a person, development will be limited. Is the same true of settings? Bronfenbrenner suggests so, as we will see in several hypotheses and propositions as we continue.

Ecological transitions provide the person opportunities or challenges to adapt to the new setting or role. As the person gains experience in more roles and more settings, does the person's view of the ecosystem become more valid, more differentiated, and more extended? Does the person become more skilled at making such adaptations? If so, then making ecological transitions will facilitate development, and an ecosystem that affords opportunities for ecological transitions will foster development.

The way a person manages ecological transitions might also provide an assessment of the person's developmental status, or maturity. In Section 5, on Activities, we considered Proposition B, that a person's developmental status might be indexed by the nature of the molar activities the person engages in without direction. With this proposition in mind, we might ask how the person *prepared* for an anticipated transition, such as moving from home to college. How *accurate* was the person's understanding of what college would be like? Did the person *seek out* information about the setting and the roles, relations, and activities that would be expected there? Did the person talk to other informed people about adapting to the transition? Once in the new setting, did the person have the skills to manage his or her participation in the pattern of the microsystem, engage in the activities there and form appropriate relationships? As we proceed we will encounter other aspects of experience in the ecosystem that may contribute to a person's developing ability to make ecological transitions and adapt to them well.

Is there a possibility that *too many* ecological transitions might not be good for development? Can change be too rapid? This might be the case if a transition came before the person could adapt to the preceding one, so the person could not become comfortable and skilled in the original role or setting before the next adaptation was required. Such *adaptation overload* due to an excess of transitions might hinder construction of understanding of the ecosystem and/or the skills required in it. The accumulation of the stresses of change might have undesirable effects on the person both physiologically and by depressing the person's motivation to explore and maintain the ecosystem or to engage in relationships in the new settings.

Develecology also involves tracing the *sequence of ecological transitions* a person makes. How does participation in one setting lead to or affect participation in the next setting? How are past settings and current and future settings related to each other, or similar, or different? How are the roles in a series of settings similar or different? Do we *expect* a person to move from one setting to another—elementary to middle to high school, for example? What settings are *available* in a person's ecosystem for the person to transition into? We will focus on these questions in Section 16 as we examine Developmental Trajectories.

As we proceed, we will also consider other ways ecological transitions occur. Are they chosen or forced upon the person? Is the person prepared for them? Are they made alone or with others? What features in new settings help or hinder the person's adaptation to them? When the ecological transition involves a new role, what preparation or training does the person have, and how is playing the new role supported by others in the setting?

In general, *ecosystems are facilitating* when the ecological transitions that happen in them offer the developing person new roles and new settings that involve activities and relationships that will contribute to development. The new roles and activities and relationships will be supported by others in both the old and the new settings. The developing person will be engaging in increasingly complex activities, a greater variety of roles, and relations that have positive affect, high levels of reciprocity, and increasing power for the developing person. You will recognize these concepts from previous sections, illustrating that we are constructing a system of interrelated concepts that all help to describe how the ecosystem shapes a person's development. In the next section, we will review the important characteristics of systems, so we can be sure we are thinking appropriately about them.

Remember: Ecological transitions always involve change in a role or a setting, or both, and you should be able to specify the changes involved.

Reference

Bronfenbrenner, U. (1979). *The Ecology of Human Development: Experiments by Nature and Design*. Cambridge, MA: Harvard University Press.

11

ESSENTIALS OF SYSTEMS THEORY

Every human setting contains a system. A system is defined as "components that function or operate together." The components of a system are connected in some *functional* way so that if one is operating, others will tend to operate too. Changes in the way one component operates will change the way the other components operate. In a system, the action or operation of any element affects the others—not always, but at least potentially. If an element is never affected by the operation or action of any other part, and if it does not affect the others, then the element arguably is not part of the system, or at least not a functional part of the system.

As a simple example, an automobile is a *mechanical* system, with a human component, the driver. If you press on the accelerator in a car, the fuel pump sends more fuel into the cylinders, which fire more quickly, turning the crankshaft faster, etc., and making the car go faster. If you step on the brake at the same time, the cylinders fire more quickly, but there is more resistance to overcome because you're pushing the brake pedal, so the engine turns faster, but the car doesn't move more quickly. The actions of the driver, the functions of the accelerator and fuel system, and the operation of the braking system all affect the speed of the engine and the forward movement of the car. The nature of the roadway under the car will also affect the forward movement of the car, depending on whether it is uphill or down, deep mud, or icy.

Human *social* systems also are made up of components—people—who behave in particular ways, or engage in activities related to their roles. When one person speaks to another, the other tends to listen and respond. If they occupy the roles of parent and child, when the child says, "I'm hungry," the parent may respond by preparing food. In most social systems, a pattern of activities and relationships and roles is fairly quickly established. The longer the people in the system live or work or play together, the more stable the system is likely to become. The more stable and enduring the system, the more it resists change. People tend to fall into the familiar comfortable routines and habits of relating to each other.

When a person who is normally present is absent from the system, the system functions differently. The system also changes when a new person enters it. When any person in a system changes significantly, the system changes, though the others in the system are likely to resist change initially. Family systems theories focus and elaborate on the complexities and implications of these intrinsic characteristics of human systems.

Mechanical systems are static, or fixed. Changes in them often signal problems. Human social systems are not mechanical. Rather they are *living* systems, or dynamic, organic, or learning systems. Such systems change. They change because the components change. People develop, and their functions change as they adapt to their own changes. As people change, the system seeks stability or homeostasis. Living systems also change because events happen in the larger systems they are embedded in. As the surrounding system changes with the passage of time, a living system adapts to those changes as well.

In *ecological* theories, the environment is also an important part of the system. While some living systems may tend to operate in their typical fashion wherever they are, others are dependent on the environment in which they occur. The ecosystem *includes* and is *specific to* a particular location and its physical features. Why is this so? Because the physical features of a setting define what activities can take place in it (Proposition F). In biology, a pond ecosystem exists in and around a pond, and is different from a desert ecosystem. The pond and the desert are different physical environments and support different organisms and relationships among them. So, too, with the human ecosystem. Human ecosystems exist in different settings and include different people. Many of the settings most important in human development come with their own sets of roles and activities and relations, their own meanings. Consider home, school, your workplace, a hospital, a summer camp, a place of worship. Each of these settings is loaded with literal and symbolic meanings, expectations, limits, possibilities, etc. And each is distinctly different in the way it is built, the activities that are possible and impossible in it, the roles we expect it to contain, and the ways participants behave in the setting. Each contains a unique or distinct **microsystem**.

At the same time, a person's ecosystem usually extends well beyond any particular setting, to include a large number of settings, each containing a different microsystem, and among all of them, a wide variety of microsystems. The settings are not isolated from each other, however, but are connected to each other in several ways. Thus, a person's ecosystem includes a number of settings integrated into a system of relationships *among* the settings.

In the following sections, we will examine Bronfenbrenner's analysis of the ecosystem. The ecosystem is the whole—all the elements that are related to or experienced by the developing person. Bronfenbrenner differentiates the ecosystem into *several subsystems—microsystem, mesosystem, exosystem,* and *macrosystem.* Each subsystem has specific elements and characteristics. Each is a system of components and processes. Each has specific relationships to the others. Change in any one is likely to be associated with change in one or more of the others. Combined, the subsystems make up the entire ecosystem for a person.

Throughout the following sections, you will encounter similarities and parallels between the systems, but there will also be differences. The parallels are a very important feature of Bronfenbrenner's framework, in which the various subsystems follow similar principles. Be careful to keep in mind the *crucial differences* among the subsystems. As I wrote in Section 3, the microsystem, mesosystem, exosystem, macrosystem, and chronosystem are *not* like a set of nesting Russian dolls. They are not identical but different in size. They are not simply encased in each other. Each subsystem is different, each is related differently to each of the others, and each is a separate, unique, and indispensable component of the ecosystem.

Remember: When we refer to a system, we should be able to specify the component parts that compose it and how they relate to each other. When we describe a system, we should try to understand how the system functions, generally, as well as under different conditions. We should attempt also to specify the places or locations where the system is found, as the setting is a part of the system. Whenever change happens in any part of a living system, the entire system must adapt to the change in some way. Remember too, that whenever we are *in* an ecosystem, we are *part of* the ecosystem, one of its elements.

12

MICROSYSTEM

In develecology, every setting contains a system, the smallest system in which the person participates, and thus, a **MICRO** system. Each microsystem is made up of people, their activities, their relations with each other, and the roles they play. Specifically, in Bronfenbrenner's view, the microsystem is defined this way:

> A **microsystem** is a pattern of activities, roles, and interpersonal relations experienced by the developing person in a given setting with particular physical and material characteristics.
>
> *(DEFINITION 2, Bronfenbrenner, 1989, p. 227)*

Note three key features of this definition. First, the microsystem is the *pattern* of the components. A system, as described above, is more than its parts. A system is a group of interacting, interrelated, or interdependent elements forming a complex whole. The *elements* of the microsystem are people, their activities, their roles, and their relationships. The microsystem is the pattern they create, how they are organized within the setting. The notion of **system** refers to how things are connected and relate and transact with each other. System refers to the *process* of the organized whole, not just to the individual parts. System is abstract, dynamic. To understand a system, particularly a human or social system, we have to see it in operation.

The second key feature of the definition is that what is important about the microsystem are those aspects of it *as experienced by the developing person*. The microsystem is the pattern as experienced by the person whose development we are interested in. There may be some parts of the pattern we, as objective observers, might think important, but for Bronfenbrenner, if they are not part of the focus person's experience, they are not part of the person's microsystem. They are not likely to impact development directly. For example, does this mean that parents' sexual activities that take place when a child is asleep are not part of the child's *microsystem*? Perhaps. But as they are likely to affect the parents' interactions with the child, they may be still part of the child's **ECO***system*.

The third key feature of the definition is that the *microsystem exists in a setting* with definable physical and material characteristics. These characteristics of the setting help to determine what activities can take place in the setting, and what the pattern can be. This is Proposition F, discussed earlier in Section 9, on settings.

Return for a moment to the second key feature, and think about its implications. If the microsystem is the pattern experienced by the developing person, what happens if there are several people in the system? Does each of them experience a different microsystem? Yes, in Bronfenbrenner's view. And that is an essential point in understanding the ecosystem. In fact, each person has a unique ecosystem, in which he or she is the center, the starting point for defining the personal ecosystem. Each person's ecosystem is defined *relative to the individual*, the person Bronfenbrenner refers to as the "developing person." While other approaches to the human environment refer to the ecosystem as if there is one we all participate in, Bronfenbrenner's scheme focuses on the individual's ecosystem. The individual ecosystem is the one we must understand to explain a particular person's development. In that ecosystem, the person is adapting to or learning to understand the microsystems that are experienced. We each have a unique ecosystem that *overlaps* with the ecosystems of other people, but is *not identical* to anyone else's. I may play a role in your ecosystem, but our ecosystems are different.

As an example of unique microsystems within a setting, consider a household with two parents and two children. Using Bronfenbrenner's definition, each of the four would experience a different system. Why? Well, if we assume the parents were a married heterosexual couple, one parent would have a husband, while the other would have a wife. Both would have two children. The two children both would have two parents, but unless they were twins, one of them would have an older sibling, while the other would have a younger sibling. So, the *pattern* of relationships each person *experiences* would be *different*, and the pattern of relationships is part of the larger pattern of the microsystem.

To recapitulate: The microsystem is the *pattern* of *activities* (what you do), *roles* (who does what, e.g., mother, child, teacher, student), and interpersonal *relations* (how each relates to and feels about the others) in a setting. A setting is a place that can be defined and described, whose characteristics determine what is likely to happen there. And the perspective is the individual person's. Figure 12.1 illustrates a microsystem and its components in a setting.

Microsystems can be compared and differentiated. How do two microsystems you participate in differ from each other? Do you participate in two similar microsystems? We will need to come back later to consider the ways the microsystems of each sort are similar within a particular culture. Those similarities or consistencies across settings of a particular type are features of the *macrosystem*, the most abstract level in Bronfenbrenner's scheme. (Most abstract, but not the largest. The largest level is the entire *ecosystem*.)

When we look for a *pattern*, what do we mean? Bronfenbrenner is not specific about what he means by *pattern*. The word has many meanings, and there are many possible kinds of patterns, or arrangements, of the components of the microsystem. The essence of all microsystem patterns is that the components—the roles, relationships, and activities—are related to each other. How are they related in this particular microsystem, in this particular setting? What roles are connected to which activities, and what relations engage in which activities? How does change in one affect the others? How do they change across time, for example, through a day, or a week, or the seasons? Is the pattern stable across time, or does it change? How does a change in a role, or relation, or activity, or who is present, change the pattern? There is no specific kind of pattern that is always present or that has to be analyzed in each case. In every microsystem, however, the developing person is experiencing *some* kind of pattern of the three elements. The pattern depends on who is present and on the specific physical characteristics of the setting.

The Microsystem and Development

Now we need to connect the microsystem to development. How is the pattern of roles, relationships, and activities experienced by the developing person important in the process of developing? Let's remind ourselves of what development means to Bronfenbrenner:

> Development is the process through which the growing person acquires a more extended, differentiated, and valid conception of the ecological environment, and becomes motivated and able to engage in activities that reveal the properties of, sustain, or restructure that environment at levels of similar or greater complexity in form and content.

The developing person in the microsystem is participating in a web of roles, relations, and activities. The person is actively engaged in activities, actively relating to others in the system, actively filling a role and experiencing the roles filled by the other people. The person is in the process of constructing an understanding of the world of that microsystem, and perhaps adapting to it, or over time, functioning effectively in it. Additionally, the person may be constructing an understanding of the world of *other* microsystems she experiences, if the one she is in includes information about or interpretations of the world outside the current setting.

The roles and relations and activities in the microsystem are the stuff or ingredients of the experience from which the person is constructing knowledge and skills. The pattern of roles, relationships, and activities has characteristics that promote development of particular knowledge and/or skills. The setting is where development takes place. The microsystem is where the processes of development happen, as the developing person attempts to make sense of and become competent in the specifics of her/his environment.

Bronfenbrenner notes that as we try to understand a microsystem, we must take into account *everybody* present in the setting, including the observer, whose presence will change the microsystem from its typical pattern when the observer is not present (Proposition D, 1979, p. 66).

Whether a microsystem will facilitate development depends on how each of its components—activities, roles, and relations—facilitates development separately, as well as on how the *pattern* operates to promote development. Do the relations support engaging in molar activities, do the relations support each other, do the relations support engaging in and with the various roles contained in the microsystem? Are the various roles compatible or complementary, as opposed to conflicting or hindering? Does the pattern permit time for joint molar activities, for exploring roles, and for positive affect in the relations? Do the activities in the microsystem become more complex over time? Do the relations involve increasing power for the developing person?

If the answer to many of the questions in the preceding paragraph is "no," then we have evidence that a particular microsystem is not good for development. Here it is important to point out that people participating in such an environment may still adapt to it, learn what is expected, and become comfortable in it. In this way, adapting to a setting and its microsystem may be detrimental to one's development. A person may be very comfortable and very well accepted in a microsystem, but that is quite different from developing in that microsystem. While the concept of microsystem might seem relatively simple, the variety of potential patterns is very great. When viewed as they change across time, describing microsystems and their relation to development may become very complex.

A *developmentally facilitating microsystem*: Review the concepts of activity, relation, and role we have discussed so far, and list the features of each component that might facilitate development. How might *different patterns* of those features vary in how well they facilitate development?

Remember: to describe a microsystem we have to specify the setting it is in, the roles, relationships, and activities that are contained in it, and the *pattern* of those elements that occurs across some period of time. And we need to consider the *pattern as experienced* by each person involved, or by the person whose development we are seeking to understand.

A Microsystem in a Setting

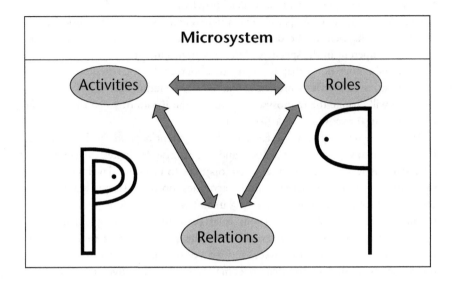

Setting

FIGURE 12.1 Microsystem and its components

References

Bronfenbrenner, U. (1979). *The Ecology of Human Development: Experiments by Nature and Design*. Cambridge, MA: Harvard University Press.

Bronfenbrenner, U. (1989). Ecological systems theory. In R. Vasta (Ed.), *Annals of Child Development, Vol. 6, Six Theories of Child Development: Revised Formulations and Current Issues* (pp. 187–249). London: JAI Press.

13

PROXIMAL PROCESSES

Enduring forms of interaction in the immediate environment are referred to as *proximal processes*. Examples of enduring patterns of proximal process are found in parent–child and child–child activities, group or solitary play, reading, learning new skills, studying, athletic activities, and performing complex tasks.

(Bronfenbrenner, 1994, p. 1644)

Proximal means close, or near. Proximal processes include *the activities a person actually engages in*. Bronfenbrenner distinguishes *proximal* processes from *distal* processes in the ecosystem. *Distal* means distant or far away. Distal processes are activities and happenings the person is not engaged in directly, those that happen in other relationships or settings away from the person. Play and study and exploration are proximal processes, if a person is doing them. Nurturing a relationship with one's parent would be a proximal process, as would learning to read. Taking something apart, painting, experimenting, reading and writing, conversing, arguing, finding problems, creating problems, and solving problems are all proximal processes. Responding to praise or punishment, cuddling on a lap listening to a story, eating or not eating your dinner, riding in a car, driving a car, repairing a car, memorizing a poem or a joke, all these are proximal processes. Proximal processes include the basic processes people engage in, such as learning, perceiving, remembering, coping with stress, and feeling emotions.

How do people develop? When do they develop? What do active organisms do that leads them to "acquire a more extended, differentiated, and valid conception of the ecological environment, and become motivated and able to engage in activities that reveal the properties of, sustain, or restructure that environment?" Why are proximal processes important in development? Bronfenbrenner answered this question about his own model, explaining

> the proposed "bioecological" model posits proximal processes as the empirically assessable mechanisms through which genotypes are transformed into phenotypes.
>
> *(1994, p. 1646)*

Bronfenbrenner implies that it is engagement in activity itself, engagement with the environment, that changes the organism, leading to understanding and skill. A *genotype* is a person's biological potentials, what is possible for the biological development of this organism. What the person actually turns into, what physical characteristics, understanding, skills, and motivation the person has, are the person's *phenotype*. Proximal processes are the activities through which the person constructs the reality from the combination of biological potentials and experiences in the environment.

Proximal Processes and the Ecosystem

A parent's relationships with co-workers in a place of employment would be a distal process for the child. They won't affect the child directly. The child won't engage in them directly or learn from them, but they may affect the father's interaction with the child, and so have an impact on the child. The actions of the legislature in authorizing funding for the child's school would be another distal process. Both distal and proximal processes are important in the ecosystem and may affect the person's development, but in different ways.

In a microsystem, the person may be conducting activities on her own—doing her own thing. An infant may be exploring, a toddler might be learning to climb, a preschooler looking through a picture book, an older child drawing, an adolescent playing music, a parent washing clothes, all these in a home setting. A grandparent may be building birdhouses, and so forth. In another kind of setting, there might be no children, but an adult might be reading a book, a librarian cataloging books, an administrative assistant reconciling financial accounts and sending bills for overdue books. Each setting has its own activities, roles, and relations. In addition, a person might be observing the activities other people engage in and possibly engaging in activities with the other people in the setting.

Development consists in part in constructing more activities and more complex and varied activities. Development also includes constructing more complex understanding of the activities we engage in and of the world we live in. The proximal processes of development depend on practice, engaging in the activities, and thinking about them. We extend and elaborate and connect our activities and knowledge, applying actions and knowledge in new situations and to new materials, gradually interrelating and integrating knowledge and actions. An implication of this is that activities will become more complex through the active engagement of the person with materials and people in the setting. The physical characteristics, the things—objects, ideas, possibilities—included in the setting make it more or less conducive to constructing more complex activities. Rich environments support more complex activities. A home without books makes literacy more difficult to construct. A nursery without manipulable materials doesn't promote fine motor skills. A setting with a flat surface and balls to kick promotes soccer skills, a classroom with materials and lab equipment is conducive to learning about science, and so on. This fact is perhaps obvious, but important to our thinking about the impact of the setting on development. The developmental potential of a setting depends on what activities one can engage in there, what one can do, both by oneself and with others.

Differences between settings mean differences between microsystems. Differences between people are a function of differences between settings and the microsystems in them. Urban apartments are different from rural farm households. Upper class homes and poverty class homes have important differences. To understand the processes of development, it is not sufficient to say that upper class homes produce different kinds of children than poverty class homes. Researchers often differentiate people using characteristics such as "class" or "subculture" or "level of education," which Bronfenbrenner refers to as *social address labels*. These labels tell you where the person "lives," so to speak, but *not what happens* there. Development is not the result of social class or level of parents' education or their occupation. Development results from the active *participation*, the *transactions* of the individual in roles, activities, and relations in a setting. Social address doesn't tell you about that participation. Social address doesn't explain how some people who grow up in poverty turn out to be very different from others who grow up in poverty.

Social address provides no guidance for how to change settings to affect development. If poverty class homes don't produce the kind of academic skills that upper class homes more commonly do, would giving poor people large amounts of money result in academic skills? Perhaps, but for those who want to understand development, carrying out such an effort would not help us understand the process. (Though it would be an interesting experiment—what Bronfenbrenner calls a "transforming experiment." How would the infusion of large amounts of money change the setting and the microsystem within it, and with what effects on the development of the participants in the setting?) To understand how and why development differs in different settings, we need to study the proximal processes occurring in the microsystem.

Changes in people change microsystems and changes in microsystems change people. It is at the heart of systems theory that if you change one person in the system, the others are going to change as well. As each person in a system undergoes developmental change, there are small or large effects on everyone else, and simultaneous effects on the activities, the relations, the roles, and ultimately the pattern of those elements that constitute the microsystem. Those changes become changes in the ecosystem that the person is adapting to and trying to understand and to maintain, so the microsystem changes are one of the engines of development. If one lived in or could live in a system in which nothing ever changed, would one develop?

People don't spend their lives in a single setting. What happens when we add a new setting to our ecosystem? How do settings compare and contrast? How do they relate to each other? What happens when a person moves from one setting to another, as may happen several times a day? Remember Bronfenbrenner's definition of an ecological transition—a change in setting or change in role, and often both.

As a person goes from setting to setting, or enters a new setting, he or she encounters a new microsystem. How does the person enter it, understand it, adapt to it? These are important questions for a developmental perspective because we often are concerned about "readiness" for a particular setting, or difficulty adapting and performing in it, or distress that accompanies a change. How well does a person cope with entrance into child care, elementary school, boarding school, or college? What happens when a person starts to participate in a youth group, a sport, a new job, goes into a nursing home, sets up housekeeping in a new apartment, retires, or is admitted to a hospital? These are all ecological transitions, and all of them involve changes in roles or settings. Each puts the person into a new microsystem.

Parenting involves preparing children for new settings and helping them adjust. Teachers deal with new children each year. A department of residential life welcomes first-year students in a university. And for each of us personally, entrance into a new setting may be a major change, a developmental milestone. Are we ready for it, and what does it mean to be ready for the transition? Can maturity be defined as the ability to enter a new setting without major distress?

It is an assumption in constructive (and perhaps other) approaches to development that a person applies the knowledge and understanding constructed from previous experiences to interpret new ones. Piaget and others believe that knowledge guides behavior. Might we think of current knowledge as the basis for a set of hypotheses about the new setting? If one has been nurtured and supported in one setting, does one expect to be nurtured and supported in a new one, and thus enter the new setting with an open and friendly attitude toward the people there? If one has been abused, then one might enter a new setting expecting to be abused, and thus be wary and tense in transactions there. Previous experience alters the way we enter a new setting. We create expectations as a way of adapting to experience and constructing its meaning. If a new setting fits our expectations, then we can adapt more easily and be comfortable. If our expectations don't fit a new setting, then we have to find a new way of understanding the new setting. When expectations don't fit, we experience disequilibrium. Mild disequilibrium results in efforts to learn, or to redefine the situation. Large disequilibrium causes stress, panic, anxiety, fear, or withdrawal. The difference between large and small disequilibrium is perhaps relative to individual temperament, intellectual skill, or flexibility. Differences in degree of disequilibrium may also reflect a person's developmental status, as suggested farther on, in Hypothesis 37 (in Section 15).

What is important in ecological transitions from familiar to new settings? Proximal processes are employed as we adapt. We observe, we study the pattern of the microsystem in the new setting, we engage in its activities, we relate to its other occupants, we may ask questions, and so forth. Further, as we enter a new setting, we may be stepping into an existing system, the microsystem in that setting. As we do so, we may be simultaneously altering that system, changing its pattern of roles, relations, and activities.

In develecology, proximal processes represent "where the rubber hits the road"—where development happens. Proximal processes create the connection between the person and experience, the central facts of learning, activity, exploration, relationships, and adaptation. As we try to understand a person's development, we will need to be mindful of the *actual* experiences of the person. What *could* have happened in the setting or what *should* have happened, or what we *assume* happened, could be quite different than what the person really experienced, and it is what the person experiences that shapes development.

An *ecosystem facilitates development* when it encourages proximal processes that lead a person to learn important skills or construct better understanding. Thus, a facilitating ecosystem provides opportunities for the person to engage in activities, such as to explore, experiment, study, compare, practice, relate, extend, think, and reflect. Proximal processes may also be involved in relations with others. These might include discussing, sharing ideas, trying to explain something, asking questions, etc. Roles might also encourage proximal processes that support development, or be defined in ways that allow those processes to happen.

Remember: a developing person is participating in an ecosystem, engaging in proximal processes, actively experiencing the ecosystem, and working to construct a more valid and differentiated understanding of the experience. The developing person is always trying to adapt to the experience and to the changes in the ecosystem, and in the process become more skilled in engaging with the environment.

References

Bronfenbrenner, U. (1979). *The Ecology of Human Development: Experiments by Nature and Design.* Cambridge, MA: Harvard University Press.

Bronfenbrenner, U. (1994). Ecological models of human development. In T. Husen & T. N. Postlethwaite (Eds.), *International Encyclopedia of Education* (2nd ed., Vol. 3, pp. 1643–1647). Oxford: Pergamon/Elsevier Science.

14

LINKS AND RELATIONS BETWEEN SETTINGS

Each setting contains a microsystem. Microsystems are contained in settings. The other three "levels" or subsystems of the ecosystem involve *relations or links between* settings. How might settings be linked to each other? How can they relate to each other?

Links between settings can be either direct or indirect.

Direct links are always people. When a person goes from one setting to another, those settings are linked by the person. If the person is the "developing person" we are focusing on, then that person is a **primary link** between the two settings. If another person also enters both the settings, the second person is a **supplementary link** between the two settings. If the developing person and the other person participate in a dyad in both settings, then the supplemental link and the primary link also are a **transcontextual or linking dyad**. A primary link creates a mesosystem, which we will study in Section 15.

Bronfenbrenner identifies three categories of *indirect links*: people, communication, and knowledge. If the developing person participates in one setting, while another person participates in both that setting and another setting that the developing person does *not* go into, then the second person is an **intermediate link** between the two settings for the developing person. So intermediate links connect settings the developing person goes into *indirectly* to settings the developing person does not go into. Farther on, we will see that these intermediate links create another level of the ecosystem that is referred to as the *exosystem*.

Another kind of indirect linkage between settings is communication of any sort between two settings, or **intersetting communication**. Intersetting communications are "messages transmitted from one setting to the other with the express intent of providing specific information to persons in the other setting."

Typical forms of intersetting communication are telephone conversations, e-mail, snail mail, announcements, and messages carried back and forth by people. Communication of some sort, or prior experiences of people involved in both settings may create another kind of indirect link, **intersetting knowledge**. Intersetting knowledge "refers to information or experience that exists in one setting about the other. Such knowledge may be obtained through intersetting communication or from sources external to the particular settings involved, for example, from library books" (1979, p. 210).

Bronfenbrenner does not specify whether intersetting knowledge must exist in both settings, or only in one. It may be useful to think about the different *types of knowledge* that could form indirect links between settings. For example, settings might be linked by:

- mutual awareness of the people in each setting;
- knowledge about one setting held by occupants of a second, with or without complementary knowledge of the second setting existing in the first;
- knowledge in both settings created by communication and by travel between the two settings by direct links between the settings.

Figure 14.1 summarizes the types of links and the kinds of settings they connect.

In an ecosystem, settings may be isolated from each other, with no links, or they may be more or less well linked with each other. There may be one, a few, several, or many people who serve as direct links between them. There may be much communication between them. We refer to settings in an ecosystem as being sparsely or weakly linked, strongly or richly linked, or somewhere in between.

In addition to being directly or indirectly linked, *settings can be said to be related to* each other. Relations between settings are more conceptual, referring to comparison or analysis of the settings. Settings may be similar to each other, or different. They may be congruent with each other. They can be in conflict with each other. The people involved in the settings may have attitudes about each other, based on intersetting knowledge. They may be supportive of the other setting and what happens in it, or they may be hostile to it. Keep in mind that these *relations between settings* or *attitudes about other settings* are *not links* between settings but links between settings may result in relations between or attitudes about settings.

In creating relations between settings, the kind and content of intersetting communication and intersetting knowledge are important, as are the relations among the people who are involved in the two settings. Whether the communication is one-way or two-way is a characteristic of the indirect linkage between the two settings. The content of the messages and their style influence the intersetting knowledge and the attitudes between the two settings. The

Summary of Links Between Settings	
Direct Links:	
Primary Link The Developing Person	Links two settings by participating in them
Supplemental Link Another Person	Links the same two settings by participating in them
Together, may create a transcontextual dyad	
May be supportive or non-supportive	
Indirect Links:	
Intermediate Link Another Person	Links a setting the developing person participates in to a setting the DP does not participate in
Intersetting Communication	
Intersetting Knowledge	

FIGURE 14.1   Summary of links between settings

validity of the information and the knowledge may shape the relations between the settings.

As we proceed to examine the remaining subsystems of the ecosystem, we will focus on the links and relations between settings. We will consider how (a) the kinds and numbers of links between settings and (b) the relations between settings affect development of the people in those settings. We will see that *ecosystems are more likely to facilitate development* when settings are connected by more links, and when those links are supportive of the developing person who is entering the settings, participating in the settings, or making transitions between them. In general, the more intersetting knowledge and communication there are, the more likely the ecosystem is to support a person's development.

Remember: In describing *links between settings*, Bronfenbrenner does not refer to the *physical* ways we may typically think of connecting settings—by sidewalks, phone lines, or vehicles. Again, he is focused on the *social* ecosystem— the people, their activities, and their relationships.

Reference

Bronfenbrenner, U. (1979). *The Ecology of Human Development: Experiments by Nature and Design*. Cambridge, MA: Harvard University Press.

15

MESOSYSTEM

We have considered how the pattern of activities, roles, and relations in microsystems in settings are important in shaping development. How do links and relations *between settings* add to shaping development?

The settings a person participates in and how they are linked and relate to each other constitute the *mesosystem*. "Meso" means middle, so the mesosystem is not the smallest subsystem, nor is it the largest.

> The **mesosystem** comprises the linkages and processes taking place between two or more settings containing the developing person (e.g., the relations between home and school, school and workplace, etc.). In other words, a mesosystem is a system of microsystems.
>
> *(DEFINITION 3a, 1994, p. 1645)*

The mesosystem incorporates all the settings, and the microsystems they contain, *in which the person actively participates.* The mesosystem, however, is not just the collection of those settings; rather, the mesosystem is *the links and relationships among those microsystems.* **Each person has any number of microsystems, but only one mesosystem,** the mesosystem being the relationships among all the settings in which the person participates. The notion of the *meso*system attempts to account for how a person's *micro*systems relate to and affect each other.

In what sense is the mesosystem a system? What are its components and functions? The elements in the mesosystem are the *settings* the person participates in, the *links* between them, and the *relationships of the settings to each other.* How does change in one part of the system affect other parts and how the system functions?

In the preceding section, we examined what Bronfenbrenner means by relationships and connections between settings. How can microsystems that exist in different settings be connected to each other? The most important way settings in a mesosystem are connected to each other is the defining way, the way that defines what settings are in the mesosystem: the developing person participates in each of them. Therefore, the person connects the settings by going into and out of each of them, and is thus the *defining* and *primary* link among them (1979, p. 209).

There can be more than one primary link between two settings. This happens when two particular settings are in the mesosystems of two different people. Since both people pass between the same two settings, there are two primary links between the settings. These multiple primary linkages mean that the same two people participate in both settings, with each other. If they are aware of each other, they are then a "transcontextual dyad," because the dyad exists in or crosses more than one setting or context. Such transcontextual dyads create a network of settings and people who share them—a "first-order" network. For each individual, the other person is also a "supplemental link" between the two settings. There may be additional supplemental links between settings—other persons who participate in both settings.

Settings in a mesosystem also may be linked by **intersetting communication** and **intersetting knowledge**, as described in the previous section. The types of linkages between settings are not mutually exclusive; two settings may be linked by multiple transcontextual dyads and by one or all of the other kinds of links. The more linkages there are, the more richly or complexly the settings in the mesosystem are connected. Figure 15.1 adds links between settings to form a mesosystem in the graphic model.

A caution about usage helps in talking about one's ecosystem. A person has a single mesosystem, comprising the relations among the several microsystems he

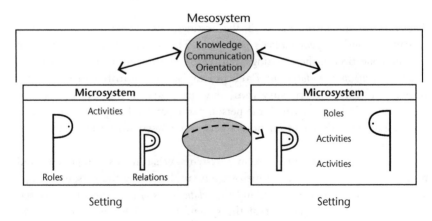

FIGURE 15.1 Mesosystem

or she participates in. So, in my one and only mesosystem, I may have several settings, each with a unique microsystem in it. When I refer to my mesosystem, I am not merely describing the settings or the microsystems in them, I am describing the relations among the settings, how they are linked, how they communicate with each other, how they are similar and different from each other.

How is the mesosystem related to a person's development? *A mesosystem supports development* when the settings are supportive of each other, and when the developing person has valid information about the settings, and vice versa. A mesosystem supports development when we move from setting to setting with people with whom we are in primary and/or developmental dyads. What settings are open or closed to a person? Which ones can a person be introduced to as a child? Which ones is a person shut out of because of race, sex, religion, or disability? What is the pattern of settings one participates in over time, and how are those settings connected? Is there a developmental sequence to the settings and activities, roles and relations the person participates in? From the preceding discussion of transitions, we can infer that a series of favorable transitions with continuing support would be helpful to development.

A person's mesosystem may *change* in two different ways. First, settings can be added to or deleted from the mesosystem. Second, the relationships between settings can change. And, of course, either adding or deleting settings in the mesosystem may change the *relationships among the other settings* in the mesosystem.

Transition into New Settings

Bronfenbrenner formulated a series of hypotheses about the features of participation in the mesosystem that shape development. Work through these, and see if you can abstract a set of mesosystem conditions that would enhance development for a person.

> The developmental potential of a setting in a mesosystem is enhanced if the person's initial transition into that setting is not made alone, that is, if he enters the new setting in the company of one or more persons with whom he has participated in prior settings.
>
> *(HYPOTHESIS 27, 1979, p. 211)*

This hypothesis refers to the situation when a person *adds a new setting* to the mesosystem by entering that setting for the first time. Hypothesis 27 emphasizes the importance of supplemental links. Why would supplemental links be helpful? What is likely to happen if people have experience in the same settings, and know the same people?

When the person starts to participate in and adapt to the new setting, the microsystem in it may support development, or not. (Remember that the microsystem is the pattern of roles, relationships, and activities in the setting.) Within the new setting, all the hypotheses about how roles, relations, and dyads facilitate development are pertinent. But now that this new setting and its microsystem are in the person's mesosystem, we need a new set of hypotheses to direct our thinking about the differences and similarities between the old setting(s) and the new setting. Did previous settings the person has participated in prepare her for the new setting? How does the microsystem in a previous setting compare to the microsystem in the new one? How do the two microsystems relate to the person, and how do they relate to each other, that is, how do the people in the two settings regard each other?

Similarities and Differences Among Settings

To capture such questions, Bronfenbrenner focuses on varieties of similarities and differences between settings, and between the microsystems in the settings. He also raises the importance of intersetting knowledge, and perhaps "intersetting attitude." In Hypothesis 28 (1979, p. 212), he says the settings will promote development if:

- the microsystem in each has similar or compatible expectations, or "role demands" for the developing person;
- the microsystems in the settings encourage the people in each setting to trust and regard the other settings positively; and
- the people in the two settings agree about developmental goals for the person (goal consensus); and
- encourage progress toward balance of power that favors the developing person.

Like many of the hypotheses, Hypothesis 28 incorporates several different concepts or components. Sorting out the implications of the hypothesis requires breaking it down it into its components to understand the whole complex set of circumstances referred to. In this hypothesis, Bronfenbrenner specifies at least *three conditions that will help a child's development*:

1 The first condition is that the *role demands* among the settings are compatible.

What are role demands? Role demands would include most centrally, the behaviors expected of the person in the role. Compatible means that the roles expected of the person in the two microsystems don't interfere or conflict with each other. Compatible may also mean that practicing a role in one of the settings won't lead the person to be unable to perform a different role well in the other setting. For example, if a child is expected to be loud and boisterous at home and avoid quiet pursuits, such as reading, while teachers at school expect the child to be polite and self-controlled, and to sit and read for long periods of time, we could say the demands for the role of child were *not* compatible between the two settings. (Keep in mind that being *similar* is not the same as being *compatible*.)

2   The second condition is that the *roles, activities, and dyads the person engages in* (the elements of the microsystem) *in each setting*, encourage three attitudes: developing mutual trust, positive orientation, and goal consensus *between the settings*. *Trust* is based on intersetting knowledge, *positive orientation* is an attitude or affect, and *goal consensus* might refer to the views of the ecosystem held by the various participants in each setting, and what they see as desirable for the development of the person being considered.

3   The third condition is that the microsystem in each setting encourages the balance of power between the person and others in the settings to gradually favor the developing person. The *evolving balance of power* is familiar from the discussion of the ways dyads contribute to development.

These conditions are repeated in several of the hypotheses, each time being attached to a different aspect of the mesosystem. It will be important always to be sure to *incorporate what happens in both, or all, the settings* in the portion of the mesosystem under consideration.

Keep in mind that Hypothesis 28 is about the mesosystem, the relations between two settings. The developing person participates in the microsystem in each of the settings. So, the important considerations are whether the microsystem in each setting encourages attitudes of trust *toward the other* setting, positive orientation *toward* the other setting, goal consensus *between* the settings, and an evolving balance of power in favor of the developing person *in the other setting*. Whether the *microsystem* in each setting supports the development of the person is a separate, but different, matter. Hypothesis 28 is about how each microsystem supports the relationship *between the settings*.

Note as well that Hypothesis 28 echoes Hypothesis 4. Each suggests that gradual shift in the balance of power toward the developing person is good for the person's development. Hypothesis 4 refers to the balance of power in any dyad, while Hypothesis 28 suggests that the microsystem in a setting can encourage that shift in balance of power to happen in the dyads in *another* setting. That different hypotheses about different elements of the ecosystem parallel each other using similar language may seem repetitive and redundant. True, they are repetitive, but they are not truly redundant, since each refers to a different element of the system. Generating different hypotheses is Bronfenbrenner's way of isolating and focusing on specific features of the ecosystem that may be important. What the similarity across the concepts and the hypotheses means is that the system Bronfenbrenner constructed is internally consistent, with the same principles applying across all levels. That consistency contributes to the great power of his formulation.

Number and Variety of Settings

Another example of the parallel principles is represented in other propositions and hypotheses about the mesosystem. Remember that earlier, Proposition 1 and Hypotheses 1, 14, and 19 referred to the importance to development of the number and variety of activities, roles, and relations the developing person participates in. In Hypothesis 29 (1979, p. 212) Bronfenbrenner applies the same principle to the number and variety of settings the person participates in. He suggests that engaging in more different settings is good for development, especially if the settings make developmental dyads likely. In Hypothesis 30 (1979, p. 213) he suggests that diversity among the settings a person participates is good, and identifies diversity among participants in the settings, such as ethnic background, socio-economic status, religion, age, and other demographic features.

Thinking back to the earlier hypotheses we can see why these hypotheses about the mesosystem might be valid. If development is enhanced by engaging in and with a variety of roles, and by participating in a variety of complex molar activities, these are more likely to happen if one is active in a variety of settings representing a variety of different types of people. In another parallel connection to Bronfenbrenner's definition of development, engaging in the variety of types of settings mentioned will likely lead the person to develop a more differentiated and valid understanding of the surrounding world.

Shared Settings

Sharing settings with people—supplemental linkage—is also important in development, as reflected in several hypotheses. These hypotheses all refer to transcontextual dyads, that is, to the relations a person participates in that occur in more than one setting. When two people are involved with each other in more than one setting, they represent a direct link and a supplemental link between the settings. Bronfenbrenner appears to assume that sharing settings with other people has advantages for the developing person over time. He hypothesizes that the more experience a person has as part of transcontextual dyads, the better able the person will be to benefit from a new developmental experience (Hypothesis 31, 1979, p. 214). He elaborates on this by suggesting that if one's culture (or perhaps one's family) encourages transcontextual dyads, one will be more able to benefit from new experiences (Hypothesis 32, 1979, p. 214). And in Hypothesis 33 (1979, p. 214) he adds that children's development will be facilitated by encouraging them to maintain transcontextual dyads across multiple different settings.

Why would transcontextual dyads facilitate development? These hypotheses rely on the connection between experience and development: engaging in new experiences provides opportunities to construct a more differentiated view of the world. The more experiences one has, the better one will understand the world, and thus the more likely one will be to understand and profit developmentally from the next experience. Bronfenbrenner assumes that transcontextual dyads are likely to engage in some proximal processes that contribute to development. What would those processes be? People who share settings and experiences are more likely to discuss, analyze, and elaborate on those experiences with each other. They "carry" their shared experiences across settings with them and discuss or use them in other settings. And that discussion may encourage comparison and differentiation of experiences, leading to better, more valid, understanding of one's world.

The value of the supplemental link—the other person in the transcontextual dyad—depends on the link's specific relationship to the developing person and what that person does in the settings they share. Remember Hypothesis 28 and the conditions that determine whether settings in a mesosystem support development (see pp. 74–75). If the participation of the supplemental link encourages the settings to meet those conditions, that will be good for the development of the developing person. We call supplemental linking persons who do that, **supportive links**. Supportive links improve the mesosystem's capacity to facilitate development (Hypothesis 34, 1979, p. 214).

Hypothesis 34 parallels Hypothesis 28. Hypothesis 28 refers to the microsystems as the *developing person* engages in them, while Hypothesis 34 refers to the ways the *supportively linking person* engages in them.

The *number of supportive links* there are between settings also influences the potential of a mesosystem. The more there are, the higher the potential, and the fewer there are, the lower the potential (Hypothesis 35, 1979, p. 215).

I said above that the relationship in the transcontextual dyad is also important. People with whom the developing persons have primary dyads have more supportive influence on development than others, and their influence is even greater if they engage in joint activities and primary dyads with other people in the settings, in addition to the developing person (Hypothesis 36, 1979, p. 215).

These preceding hypotheses assume that when the other people involved in the settings have enduring, more extensive, reciprocal, and more complex relations, they are more likely to care about and promote the development of the person who is the primary link in the mesosystem.

This discussion suggests more broadly that there are aspects of the ecosystem that encourage supportive links and developmental potential. An ecosystem could also *discourage* supplemental links and supportive links. There might then be few supplemental links, or the ones that exist might be non-supportive and detrimental links.

Supplemental Links May Be Less Important as the Person Develops

The hypotheses referred to above imply that developing people benefit from supplemental and supportive links as they experience their mesosystem settings. If development consists of better understanding and increasing competence in the ecosystem, what might be the effect of continuing development on the importance of supplemental links in a mesosystem? Might it be that a person could reach a point where it is important to test her competence and understanding by undertaking a new experience on her own? Bronfenbrenner considers that in a hypothesis in which he suggests that the positive effects of supplemental links might be greatest for people with less competence (e.g., young children, newcomers, people who are ill) and decrease as the person develops more competence. As the person becomes more competent in her own ecosystem, development might be more greatly facilitated by experiences of entering new settings with no supplemental links (Hypothesis 37, 1979, p. 215).

Bronfenbrenner here suggests that if a person has developed sufficiently, the support provided by transcontextual dyads and supportive links might not be necessary, or even particularly helpful. This might happen if the person's experiences across settings in the mesosystem have led to a valid, differentiated, and extended understanding of the world, as well as sufficient practice in adapting to new situations that the person is skilled in figuring out and adapting to the microsystem in any new setting. This hypothesis is consistent with his Proposition B, that a measure of a person's developmental status, or maturity, might be the variety and complexity of the molar activities the person engages in on her own.

In this discussion, keep in mind that *supplemental links are direct links*—people—so "supportive link" here refers to a person. Indirect links, whether intersetting communication or intersetting knowledge, also can be *supportive of development*, but they are not supplemental links.

Indirect Links

Now we'll consider the indirect links among settings in a mesosystem. Indirect links are not people; they include intersetting communication and intersetting knowledge. Again, we'll start with a parallel to previous hypotheses. This time, in Hypothesis 38 (1979, p. 216), where Bronfenbrenner proposes that indirect links will support development if they encourage the conditions of the mesosystem that support development—trust, positive orientation, and agreement between settings about goals, and shifts in power toward the developing person. Remember that mutual trust, positive orientation, goal consensus, and a balance of power are not *links* between settings; they are *relations* between settings, ways settings are compatible or congruent with each other, or attitudes people in one setting have about the other setting. Communication between settings happens in a variety of ways. Communication between settings is more likely to promote development if it is easy to do, extensive, and two-way, going in both directions between settings. For children, it should include communication from and to the family (Hypothesis 39, 1979, p. 217). Direct communication between settings is more likely to be two-way, and is more likely to support development. Communication that is more personal is more likely to be clearer, and will support development better. Face-to-face communication allows each participant to see and hear the non-verbal components of the communication, as well as making it easier for each to ask for more information. Bronfenbrenner lists possible forms of communication in order from more to less personal: face-to-face, personal letter or note, phone, business letter, announcement (Hypothesis 40, 1979, p. 217).

BOX 15.1

Bronfenbrenner constructed Hypothesis 40 well before the emergence of modern technological media. Where in his ordered list of modes of communication would you place newer modes, such as texting, video chat, tweets, and posting on other social media?

Effective communication between settings creates intersetting knowledge. Direct links, people participating in two or more settings, construct their own knowledge about settings from their experience, and carry it with them as they pass from one setting to another. They may share it with other people, communicating their knowledge, leading people in the second setting to construct their own knowledge about the first setting. In these ways, intersetting knowledge is created. Communication between settings is another way intersetting knowledge is created. How do intersetting communication and knowledge facilitate development? Hypothesis 41 addresses the conditions under which people enter a new setting:

> Development is enhanced to the extent that, prior to each entry into a new setting the person and members of both settings involved are provided with information, advice, and experience relevant to the impending transition.
>
> *(HYPOTHESIS 41, 1979, p. 217)*

Bronfenbrenner supposes that with better advance knowledge and understanding, people are more likely to act appropriately in a new setting, respond more appropriately to each other, and thus experience more positive affect and greater reciprocity in the microsystem of the new setting. Advance knowledge and previous experience suggest the person enters the new setting with a more valid and differentiated view of what will be expected in the new setting, and with better skills to adapt to those expectations.

Hypothesis 41 refers to information provided *before* an ecological transition occurs. Hypothesis 42 (1979, p. 217) focuses on what happens after the initial entry into a setting. It proposes development in the new setting will depend on the accuracy or validity of the communication and how often it is updated. That communication will determine the *intersetting knowledge* that is available *after the person enters the new setting*. Presumably, that knowledge will affect the level of trust, positive attitude, and mutual support between the two settings. Can you think of examples that would support this hypothesis?

Shared Activity Networks

Elaborating on the importance of supportive links, joint activities, and multiple settings, Bronfenbrenner considers a special kind of mesosystem with significance in development. In Hypothesis 43 (1979, p. 223), he regards more deeply the *importance of experiences shared with other people*. Coming to understand experiences and learn from them is facilitated by discussing them with each other. Discussing experience is a proximal process important in development. Since each person may have a somewhat different perspective on the experience, comparing and reflecting together increases the validity and differentiation of each person's understanding. Additionally, sharing experiences over time, in more than one setting, allows people to compare and contrast settings and experiences in them. Sharing experience across time makes it possible to note and discuss change in the ecosystem and in each other. Bronfenbrenner identifies a particular mesosystem, or portion of overlapping mesosystems, in which a group of people all participate in joint activities with each other in multiple settings. In this network of settings, developmental potential is great, if the developing person gradually experiences an increase in power relative to the other members, toward balance.

Bronfenbrenner labeled this segment of overlapping mesosystems a "closed activity network" (1979, p. 223). "Closed" sounds negative to our ears, but here *it doesn't mean bad*; it's just descriptive. Students sometimes misunderstand this to mean the people involved have no other settings in their mesosystems, which also is not his meaning. To help avoid confusion I substitute the phrase "*shared activity network.*" The people in a shared ("closed") activity network also participate in incomplete or open social networks.

Why would sharing the same parts of a mesosystem, or creating a "shared activity network" be helpful to a person's development? Perhaps if *all* the activities and relations a person engaged in were within a shared activity network, that might be bad. But if it means that the person engages in *some* joint activities in the same primary dyads across settings (transcontextual primary dyads), then there will be more opportunity for discussion of the activities and extension of them, and for constructing shared understanding of the ecosystem. The people who share the activities can engage in proximal processes based on the shared experience. They can "process" the experience, as we say. They can compare and contrast settings and roles, ask and answer questions, and enhance understanding for each other. By engaging in these proximal processes, the participants in the "shared activity network" are constructing more valid and differentiated understanding of their experience and their ecosystem, which *is* development, as Bronfenbrenner defines it.

Bronfenbrenner is not suggesting one's entire mesosystem should be a shared activity network. The part of it that is, however, may be particularly conducive to development. Healthy shared activity networks are significant in the creation of family ties and other group bonds. A family group that shares activities in a home, goes to religious activities together, engages in recreational activities, and takes vacations together would represent such a potentially beneficial system. On the other hand, Bronfenbrenner hypothesizes that the mesosystem also should be "open" to additional settings and activities. We might consider whether early in life an infant might participate in a small shared activity network, and very few other settings. As the child's mesosystem expands, there might be more unshared settings, and perhaps several small shared activity networks, one with family members, another with peers, and so forth.

In his discussion of mesosystems, Bronfenbrenner also offers one last hypothesis that considers the importance of settings where developing people may not be in the company of family members. In Hypothesis 46, he suggests that it will foster development to have increasing access to settings where the child can be engaged in responsible joint activities with more developed people who are not her parents (1979, p. 282). Such activities increase the probability the child will participate in developmental dyads, and the hypothesis connects to earlier hypotheses regarding the importance of multiple complex activities, relations, and role repertoires.

BOX 15.2

Try describing your current mesosystem. What are the settings you participate in? How are the settings linked? Are the linkages weak or strong, sparse or rich? Do your various microsystems support each other, or conflict with each other? Can you draw your mesosystem?

Think back to the earlier discussion of complex settings, such as universities. We suggested that such institutions might be considered settings, or settings with sub-settings. If we consider a university to be the latter, then we can think about it as containing a mesosystem of relationships among those sub-settings. As implied before in the discussion of settings, whether we choose to describe them as settings or mesosystems of settings depends on the level of our analysis and our purpose. One of the strengths of Bronfenbrenner's concepts and principles is that they are flexible, making them more practically useful.

In develecology, *a mesosystem will support development* to the extent:

1   there are linkages and they are supportive;
2   the microsystem in each of the settings supports the others and supports the developing person's activities, roles, and relations;
3   the settings are varied; and
4   the transcontextual dyads provide opportunity to discuss, share, question, extend, and validate the person's understanding of all the experiences he or she engages in.

A developmentally facilitating mesosystem will be richly linked, in multiple ways, shared by people who support a person's development, and offering diverse settings and experiences.

Many of the hypotheses about the mesosystem have an important implication for develecologists. For example, in the wording of Hypothesis 33, Bronfenbrenner refers to "providing experiences" to promote development. This raises an important possibility in Bronfenbrenner's view, the possibility that *development might be altered* by changing specific aspects of the person's ecosystem. Bronfenbrenner is not content simply to describe and specify the particular features of an ecosystem. His broader purpose is to guide us in our thinking about how to promote development by changing the ecosystem, a purpose directly addressing the programs and policies we create to support children and families.

BOX 15.3

You might try listing all the specific components Bronfenbrenner has identified in these hypotheses and describe how they are related to the structure and functions of the mesosystem, and how each would shape the developing person's development.

Remember: Each person has only one mesosystem. In describing a mesosystem, or part of it, it is important to specify the settings of interest, but to keep in mind that the mesosystem itself is the ways the settings are linked and relate to each other. The direct links, supplemental links and the indirect links should be identified. The attitudes and relations of settings to each other should be described. We are interested in how those links and relations *between settings* affect the development of the person whose mesosystem it is.

A common problem in working with the hypotheses related to the mesosystem is thinking of people or activities as settings, as Bronfenbrenner himself did in his original definition of the mesosystem (see Definition 3, 1979, p. 25). Friends, family, hockey, cooking, playing music, etc. are not settings. Settings in the mesosystem are definable places. Links and mesosystem relations are between the settings. Family or friends may *participate* in the microsystems in the settings, but family or friends are not the settings. Playing music or hockey may be *activities* in the microsystems in the settings, but they are not the settings. Always specify the physical settings when testing the hypotheses about the mesosystem.

References

Bronfenbrenner, U. (1979). *The Ecology of Human Development: Experiments by Nature and Design.* Cambridge, MA: Harvard University Press.

Bronfenbrenner, U. (1994). Ecological models of human development. In T. Husen & T. N. Postlethwaite (Eds.), *International Encyclopedia of Education* (2nd ed., Vol. 3, pp. 1643–1647). Oxford: Pergamon/Elsevier Science.

16

DEVELOPMENTAL TRAJECTORY

The discussion of the mesosystem in the previous section introduced the potential for looking at a person's participation in different settings across time. The characteristics of the various settings and their microsystems that a developing person engages in are related to each other in important ways. We have referred to "congruence" and "goal consensus" between settings and "increasing complexity" of activities. Let's step back and take a broader view of the mesosystem experienced as the person develops. Bronfenbrenner introduces the phrase "developmental trajectory" to refer to the result of experiences connected over time, but typically occurring in different settings.

> The developmental potential of a setting is a function of the extent to which the roles, activities, and relations occurring in that setting serve, over a period of time, to set in motion and sustain patterns of motivation and activity in the developing person that then acquire a momentum of their own. As a result, when the person enters a new setting, the pattern is carried over and, in the absence of counterforces, becomes magnified in scope and intensity. Microsystems that exhibit these properties and effects are referred to as *primary settings*, and the persisting patterns of motivation and activity that they induce in the individual are called *developmental trajectories*.
>
> *(HYPOTHESIS 47, Bronfenbrenner, 1979, pp. 284–285)*

While a person may pass through a variety of settings over the course of time, the focus of develecology is on the settings, and their microsystems, that *promote development*. Think back to Bronfenbrenner's definition of development. What experiences and transactions and activities will encourage the construction of a more complex repertoire of activities or skills? The activity might become more extended and complex in a single microsystem over a long period of time. The activity also might take place in more than one setting as the person develops. When a pattern of activity persists over a long period of time, and becomes more complex, we should be able to reconstruct its developmental history. If an interest in poetry, for example, develops and gradually becomes more and more complex, it can be referred to as a developmental trajectory. Other typical examples include competitive riding and showing of horses, figure skating, and playing varsity hockey. Each of these activities began somewhere in some simple form: horseback-riding lessons, learning to skate at age three, enjoying nursery rhymes, and so forth. Then each was practiced, and gradually integrated into more and more complex activities. This is the fate of some molar activities. If the activity persists and becomes more complex, perhaps occupying increasing amounts of the developing person's time and energy, and if it influences or directs the choices the person makes about *how* and *where* and *with whom* to spend time, in other words if it provides an element of *structure and direction* to the person's life, then it is referred to as a developmental trajectory.

The concept of a developmental trajectory integrates several elements of the ecosystem. First, a developmental trajectory refers to a *molar activity*. Second, a developmental trajectory incorporates the *settings and microsystems* where the activity occurs. Third, a developmental trajectory includes the *ecological transitions* the person has experienced over time. To understand the construction of a developmental trajectory, we need to specify the activity, look at the settings in which the activity has been practiced and elaborated, and examine the transitions from one setting to the next. What is the sequence of the settings that have influenced the trajectory? How did the microsystem in each setting support and shape the activity? Why did the transitions occur?

BOX 16.1

Consider any activity that is important to you. Where and when did it start? Who was involved in the beginning? See if you can describe the sequence of settings in which the activity occurred and how each shaped the activity. Did the activity become more complex, indicating that you were developing? Did you engage in the activity with a wider assortment of people? Did the activity lead you into new settings? Did you choose settings to enter because they supported the activity? Did you decide to stay out of some settings because they *didn't* support the activity?

If we wanted to *encourage the development* of a particular persisting pattern of an activity, such as academic interest or writing or music or horseback riding, how would we do that? Clearly, we must make it possible for the developing person to begin the activity, to engage in it over time, and for it to become more elaborated. And we must assure the developing person enters settings where the activity can be practiced, and encourage other experienced people to engage in it with the developing person.

Does the concept of developmental trajectory apply to all activities? Are there activities one could develop and persist in without entering new settings? Are there activities one could develop without engaging in the activity with other people? Perhaps, but it is a challenge to find them in real life. Once developed, an activity might persist in such a manner, without new settings, and without co-participants. As a practical matter, the behaviors and activities of interest to us developmentally probably almost universally can be analyzed using the notion of developmental trajectory.

The value of analyzing the construction of a persisting pattern of behavior and the settings in which microsystems initiate and support that pattern of behavior is that such persistent patterns of behavior include every behavior and skill we hope to encourage in development, as well as every activity we wish developing people would *not* pursue.

If a person becomes an Olympic athlete, we can understand that as the result of the creation of a developmental trajectory. If another person started in the same sport at the same time and did not become an Olympic athlete, we can examine the physical and psychological characteristics that interfered with or were incompatible with becoming an Olympic athlete. But the analysis is incomplete unless we also look at the settings that were and were not open to the person. What other activities were incompatible with the developmental trajectory? A person may be engaging in several developmental trajectories at the same time. Are they supportive of, or interfering with, each other? Asking these questions, we are examining the structure of a person's life over a par-ticular period. A develecological view encourages us to look at the individual characteristics of the person that are conducive (or not) to development on a particular trajectory, as well as looking at the microsystem features—roles, rela-tions, and activities—that support it (or not), as well as the settings that contain those microsystems. For most developmental trajectories, the meso- and exo-systems are likely to be involved as well. If one is to become an Olympic athlete, home, school, and athletic settings must be supportive of the developing trajectory.

Examining the history of settings, or the sequence of settings, a person has participated in over time gives us information about the activities, roles, and relationships a person has been exposed to. These past experiences of settings can help us understand the adaptations a person has made. Those adaptations may underlie behaviors we see later, and knowing the history may help us relate more effectively with the person, especially if the behaviors are causing problems for the person. Knowing the history also suggests the parts of the ecosystem the person has had opportunity to experience, and that may provide us better understanding of how the person views the ecosystem as well as the skills and motivations the person brings into a new setting.

The concept of developmental trajectory is particularly useful because it applies to undesirable behaviors as well as to desirable ones. As stated before, Bronfenbrenner's framework encompasses *all* development, all aspects of development, all developmental outcomes, without judgment of their desirability or social usefulness—those are macrosystem questions. For example, a life of crime represents a developmental trajectory just as much as does a life of athletic success. Becoming a heroin addict is a complex molar activity; the trajectory of addiction for any individual can be described. The child abuser has a developmental history. Becoming a doctor has a developmental trajectory, as do becoming president, an auto mechanic, a hermit, or a bank robber. Each major life activity that can be described or labeled has a developmental trajectory that can be traced through its history of settings. (While Bronfenbrenner's framework applies to all developmental trajectories, and does not require separate theories to explain undesirable outcomes, in Section 22 we will consider ways we might appropriately evaluate developmental outcomes within Bronfenbrenner's framework.)

BOX 16.2

Try the following exercise: Describe the sequence of settings in which you have participated over any period of your life. What new settings have you entered? Which have you left behind or stopped participating in? Can you describe differences among those settings over time? What would you need to focus on to describe differences? What were the roles, relationships, and activities in each, and if they were close to the same, then how might the pattern or microsystem have differed? What activities carried over from one setting to another, and how did the activities become more complex? Which activities have you continued over a long time?

Three Hypotheses about Developmental Trajectories

Three complex hypotheses explore aspects of the relationship between a mesosystem and developmental trajectories it might support. The first suggests *moving from one setting to another* might be important in the process of making apparent a person's more highly developed activities and/or understanding. If a setting has an effect on a person's development, we may not see that change in understanding, motivation, or skills right away. It may not appear until the person enters a different setting requiring some new adaptation (Hypothesis 48, 1979, p. 286).

Why would that be? Consider that the original setting might not permit new activities or roles. There might not be an opportunity to engage in the behavior or the role one is observing, while a new setting might encourage or permit the new activity or role to be practiced. How often, for example, do people change jobs because their current one doesn't offer the opportunity to use skills they have been developing? It may also be that the pattern of relations and roles in a new setting encourages a person to perform at a higher or more complex level than did the roles and relations in the prior setting.

Hypothesis 48 contains one of the most fundamental implications of a develecological perspective. It challenges an assertion often made about behavior: "The best predictor of future behavior is past behavior." Following Hypothesis 48, we must add to that assertion the qualifier: "if we assume there are no changes in the ecosystem of the person." We might also consider adding a second qualifier: "and if we assume the person does not develop." Hypothesis 48 proposes that behavior may be quite different as the person adapts to changes in the ecosystem.

The next hypothesis captures a fundamental principle in understanding differences among people and the developmental effects of social class, racism, sexism, educational inequality, ethnicity, parental support, and geography, among other factors.

> The direction and degree of psychological growth are governed by the extent to which opportunities to enter settings conducive to development in various domains are open or closed to the developing person.
>
> *(HYPOTHESIS 49, Bronfenbrenner, 1979, p. 288)*

This hypothesis brings us back to Proposition F and Proposition H, both of which are about the relation of settings to development. Why would particular settings be open or closed, or absent, in a particular child's ecosystem? How might particular "social addresses" be reflected in what settings are available?

The final hypothesis in this section raises the possibility that not all transitions from one primary setting to the next are equal in potential. Hypothesis 50 (1979, p. 288) suggests trying to tie together many of the previous concepts, particularly the notions of developmental trajectory, mesosystem, and the remaining subsystem, exosystem, to describe the development of a person's ability to enter and to make use of new settings across a life span. In this very complex hypothesis, Bronfenbrenner gives the characteristics of the two settings, current and new, that might be important in determining how the transition goes. This hypothesis might be applied to examining major ecological transitions such as adoption, changing employment, entering a new school, leaving home, and the like. The hypothesis proposes that in the transition from one setting to a new one, we can see *challenge* to the person to adapt and change, as well as *support*. The challenge comes in the new setting, and support may also be present there, as well as in the ways the new setting is connected to the old setting. If there is enough support from both, the person is likely to meet the challenge of adapting and developing. If there is too little support, the person may not be able to adapt effectively, and the developmental opportunity will be lost or reduced. If there is too much support, the person may not have to adapt, and thus the developmental opportunity will also be reduced. How much support is too much or too little? That depends on the person's developmental status and health, as well as on how well adapted and integrated the person is in the ecosystem. To assess the potential of such transitions, it is helpful to look at how developmentally facilitating previous elements of the ecosystem have been—the microsystems, mesosystem, and exosystem.

This is a challenging hypothesis, for sure. Bronfenbrenner directs us to examine the developmental trajectory the person is on and how it projects into the next setting. What kind of challenges and support have been offered in previous settings? Then we are to define the challenge represented by the next setting and the support it offers to the ongoing activity of the trajectory. Both support and challenge to adapt and to learn are needed. Is there enough support to keep the trajectory in motion? Is there enough challenge to stimulate the trajectory, to strengthen it? The *balance* between challenge and support determines whether development will be thwarted or facilitated. If there is not enough support or too much challenge, the activity can't be sustained, or motivation will be lost. If there is a high level of support, but not much challenge, the activity may not become more complex. Both the support needed and the degree of challenge effective will depend on the developmental status and personal characteristics of the developing person. Support and challenge may be offered by the new setting. They may also be offered by links and connections to previous settings, or settings entered previously, but still active. For example, family or friends may be supportive, even though they don't participate in the new setting.

As we consider these hypotheses and think of examples to illustrate them, remember that ecological transitions are potentially stressful, and require adaptation. How well prepared is the person for the challenge of adapting to the demands of a new microsystem?

An *ecosystem that supports development* will include settings and activities that support trajectories that continue across enough settings to become complex, challenging, and satisfying. The trajectories will become motivating, allow a sense of accomplishment, and perhaps a contribution to one's community. The trajectories may lead to earning a living, or to enjoyment, or both. An ecosystem supports development if developmental trajectories lead to opportunities to enter other settings, to create developmental dyads, and to share activities, understanding, and skills with other people. If an ecosystem is to support development, settings that would continue and extend a developmental trajectory should not be closed to the person, and potentially complex activities should not be cut off or ended (unless they are detrimental, of course). An ecosystem that supports development provides settings, activities, and relationships that allow alternative trajectories when a person is following an undesirable path. In this way, *developmental trajectories can be bent* toward more positive directions.

Remember: To describe a developmental trajectory, include (a) the settings in which the activity and motivation were encouraged, (b) the sequence of those settings, (c) the activity and its increasing complexity, and (d) the pattern of the person's increasing motivation to engage in the activity. To understand the developmental impact of transitions from one setting to another in the trajectory, try to describe the balance of support and challenge between the two settings.

Reference

Bronfenbrenner, U. (1979). *The Ecology of Human Development: Experiments by Nature and Design*. Cambridge, MA: Harvard University Press.

17

EXOSYSTEM

As we saw previously, the mesosystem is the relationships among the settings a person actively participates in, but there are other settings that are also important in life and in development. Bronfenbrenner incorporates those important settings in the concept of the exosystem, "exo" denoting external or outside. The settings in the exosystem are ones the developing person does not actively participate in. Settings in the exosystem are in the person's *ecosystem* because they are *linked* *to* mesosystem settings, and they affect, or are affected by, what happens in the person's mesosystem (Definition 4, Bronfenbrenner, 1979, p. 25).

In 1994, Bronfenbrenner provided the following elaboration of this definition:

> The exosystem comprises the linkages and processes taking place between two or more settings, at least one of which does not contain the developing person, but in which events occur that indirectly influence processes within the immediate setting in which the developing person lives (e.g., for a child, the relation between the home and the parent's workplace; for a parent, the relation between the school and the neighborhood peer group).
>
> *(1994, p. 1645)*

Thus, the *exosystem* refers to (a) settings a person does not participate in, but that are consequential in development, and (b) the relationships of those settings to each other and to the settings in the person's mesosystem. The settings in an exosystem have one or both of two possible connections to the person: the exosystem settings either influence what happens in the settings in which a person does participate (mesosystem settings), or what the person does influences what happens in the exosystem settings.

BOX 17.1

Can you think of examples of settings that affect you, but that you don't participate in? Can you think of settings you affect, but that you don't participate in? And are there settings you don't participate in that both affect you and are affected by you?

The components of the exosystem are particular settings and their links and relationships to each other and to mesosystem settings. The settings included in the exosystem are *not in* the person's mesosystem, but the relationships or links are between exosystem settings as well as between exosystem settings and mesosystem settings. The settings in an exosystem may be linked directly and indirectly to each other and to settings in a person's mesosystem. The relationships between settings include interconnections and influence, in both directions. Figure 17.1 adds an exosystem setting to the graphic model.

An important form of **indirect linkage** between settings *connects the exosystem to a person's mesosystem*. Recall that an **intermediate link** is created when the developing person and a second person participate in the same setting, and the second person participates in another setting that is *not* part of the developing person's mesosystem. The latter setting is linked to the setting in the developing person's mesosystem indirectly, by the participation of the other person in both. If the setting outside the developing person's mesosystem involves a third person, a person with whom the intermediate linking person interacts, this condition creates a **second-order network** of people who don't interact face-to-face, but who may know of and about each other, and who are linked by the person who does participate in both settings. While this situation of intermediate linkages may seem complex, it is the basis for our familiar conversations with new people we meet, when we try to find out if they know people we know who live or work or study in the same place the new person participates in—the "small world game."

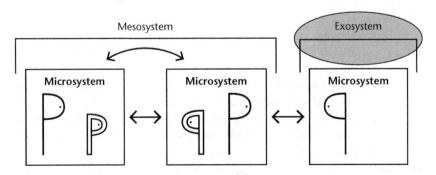

FIGURE 17.1   Exosystem and mesosystem settings

Through intermediate links, settings in a person's *meso*system and *exo*system are connected by being in someone else's mesosystem. Through intermediate links, a setting in the exosystem is a setting in the mesosystem of a person the developing person has a relation with, and vice versa.

Each individual has a unique ecosystem. Each person has a unique mesosystem, comprising the settings the person enters and participates in. The notion of trans-contextual dyads implies that mesosystems overlap. In fact, a person's mesosystem overlaps to some degree with the mesosystems of every person she has a relationship with, or with whom she shares activities or settings. But a person may not participate in all the settings in another person's mesosystem, even a very close person. A child may not go into a parent's workplace, but what happens there affects the child. Parents may not be part of the setting where an adolescent child becomes pregnant, but the adolescent's activities there affect the parent. Those settings and their impact on the developing person make up the *exo*system of the developing person. The exosystem is important in understanding development because often we are influenced by events outside our own mesosystem. A parent loses a job, a spouse has an affair, a child is injured or becomes pregnant. A school board establishes a policy that discriminates against a child, funding for health care is reduced and the clinic a child goes to is closed. A legislature creates a program for gifted children that opens new settings and opportunities to a teenager.

Power Settings

Some settings, such as legislatures and courts, may wield considerable power to influence lives, by allocating resources and making decisions about what happens in other settings. Bronfenbrenner refers to such settings as *"power settings"* (1979, p. 255). What participants in power settings do affects people indirectly by defining the laws or policies that govern an organization, community, or society, by determining what resources and how many resources are available in settings people participate in, by influencing what settings exist or which settings a person has access to, and in many other possible ways. Power settings in the exosystem are important in part because they *are* in the exosystem—people who are affected by them do not participate in them.

Settings in the exosystem are linked to a person's mesosystem in the same way settings in the mesosystem are, with the exception that the developing person is not a direct link to them. Mesosystem settings are connected to exosystem settings by *indirect links*: intermediate links (other people) and by intersetting communication and knowledge. How power settings link to mesosystem settings affects the developmental potential of the mesosystem settings. Hypothesis 44 addresses the connections:

> The developmental potential of a setting is enhanced to the extent that there exist direct and indirect links to power settings through which

participants in the original setting can influence allocation of resources and the making of decisions that are responsive to the needs of the developing person and the efforts of those who act in his behalf.

(HYPOTHESIS 44, Bronfenbrenner, 1979, p. 256)

In Hypothesis 45 (1979, p. 256) Bronfenbrenner suggests the closeness of the connections between a mesosystem setting and a power setting affects the potential developmental influences of a power setting. If a person can speak directly to a person who is active in a power setting, then there is only one step between the two, and thus the power setting is more likely to be affected by the person's words and feelings. If, on the other hand, communication must go through several different people (intermediate links), one after the other, before it reaches the power setting, the communication is likely to be less effective in influencing what happens in the power setting. Think about the popular game, "Telephone," in which players whisper a message to the next person in a circle, until it returns to the originator in often considerably altered form and meaning.

The wording Bronfenbrenner proposed for Hypothesis 45 often confuses students. It might be helpful to think of Hypothesis 45 rewritten as:

The developmental potential of a setting is greater when there are fewer *intervening steps* in the line of communication between that setting and settings of power, or separating it from settings of power.

(HYPOTHESIS 45, revised by Shelton)

The degree to which power settings influence development is a function of several factors. Do the people in the power setting have a valid view of the impact of their actions? Are they thinking about the person who will be affected by their actions? Are the interests of the developing person represented in their activities and deliberations? As we think about exosystem settings, we can anticipate that the same conditions included in Hypothesis 38, about mesosystems, may also be found to enhance developmental potential of a person's exosystem, if the intermediately linking person has similar effect there.

Develecological Advocacy

The fact that many decisions affecting our lives are made without our direct participation is the foundation for the importance of develecology in understanding social policy. Social policy is often established in power settings, and they are often in a person's exosystem. **Advocacy** is the activity of changing policymakers' and decision-makers' understanding of the world so that it includes the interests or wellbeing of the person or group advocated for. "Advocate" means to speak for, or on behalf of, another person.

A highly developed person would apply a develecological approach and manifest a highly differentiated and valid view of the ecosystem, so his or her action and decisions would benefit developing people. That would be a social or political goal of human develecology. Bronfenbrenner hypothesizes that the fewer intervening steps there are, or the more closely one is connected to power settings, the more likely people in power are to act in ways to benefit one's welfare. This is the assumption behind advocacy—to represent the developing person's interests directly. Ideally, in Bronfenbrenner's view, the developing person would participate in the decisions. In his words, "where exo- is, there shall meso- be" (1979, p. 289).

Corporations and organizations employ lobbyists to represent their interests with lawmakers. Individuals and groups make political contributions and attend fund-raising dinners so they can communicate directly with lawmakers. Campaign finance reform is intended to make it harder for the wealthy to have disproportionate influence on policy. Ethics standards for board members, lawmakers, judges, etc. are designed to minimize unfair influence. Sometimes, separation from power settings is expected. Defendants and their representatives, for example, are forbidden to communicate with and attempt to influence witnesses, judges, and juries in court proceedings. Public administrators and others are expected to reveal when they have conflicts of interest. For example, when a publicly elected lawmaker opposes or supports a law or policy that would affect directly a business in which she has an interest, the lawmaker is obligated to reveal that interest and recuse herself from the decision process.

If development is the process of constructing a more highly differentiated and valid view of one's ecosystem, then a developmental goal might be to learn where and how decisions are made that affect one's life. To construct that understanding, it would be helpful to enter those settings. It would be helpful to work to develop the skills to represent one's own interests and to influence the understanding of those who make the decisions. Examples of activities and ecosystem features that illustrate engagement in and support for development include: Student representation on school boards and university boards of trustees; shareholder attendance at corporate meetings; participation in political organizations; attendance and participation at civic and governmental hearings; informed voting; reading about administrative and legislative issues; advocating for oneself or one's child.

Special education laws were designed to allow/require hearings at which parents will be represented when decisions are made about a child with special needs. Special education regulations encourage reciprocal or two-way communication, attempting to assure that school and other officials meet and listen to parents and help parents better understand the setting of the school. This is an example of public policy attempting to encourage enhancement of intersetting knowledge and goal consensus to increase the developmental potential of a child's mesosystem.

Bronfenbrenner devoted much of his professional life to advocating for public policies and programs that take into account the developmental needs of children and their families, and that are consistent with ecological realities.

Exosystem in the Ecosystem

All the hypotheses about the mesosystem are relevant to settings in the exosystem. If a person is entering a setting in the exosystem, the person is converting that setting to a mesosystem setting, and all the hypotheses about the importance of prior knowledge, shared knowledge, transcontextual dyads, and so on, apply. In this case, the person is in the process of enlarging the mesosystem.

In develecological analysis, it is necessary to identify both the exosystem settings the person influences and the settings that influence the person's development. What happens in those settings often constitutes important *distal processes* for the developing person. The relation of what goes on in an exosystem setting to what happens developmentally in the mesosystem is often a transactional relation, with each setting influencing the other. The links and relations among exosystem settings and between exosystem settings and mesosystem settings are the same as between mesosystem settings, with the exception that the exosystem does not have the primary link created by the developing person, since the person does not enter those settings.

A *developmentally supportive ecosystem* is one in which exosystem settings are knowledgeable about and favorably regard the developing person and the people who are important in the person's life. They are supportive of the activities, relations, and settings the person participates in and may make additional settings, activities, relations, or resources available to the person. In an exosystem favorable for development, the developing person has *multiple intermediate links* and *few intervening steps* to the power settings that are influential in the exosystem. Participants in those power settings have valid and differentiated views of the ecosystem they occupy and are motivated to use their skills to improve the ecosystem in ways that support the development of other persons. They support connections among settings as well as work to create access to closed settings for those who desire to participate.

Remember: In defining a person's ecosystem, specify whether a setting is in a person's mesosystem or exosystem. A setting is not an exosystem; it is a setting *in* the exosystem. The exosystem is the settings *and* their relationship to and effects on the person or on settings in the person's mesosystem.

References

Bronfenbrenner, U. (1979). *The Ecology of Human Development: Experiments by Nature and Design.* Cambridge, MA: Harvard University Press.

Bronfenbrenner, U. (1994). Ecological models of human development. In T. Husen & T. N. Postlethwaite (Eds.), *International Encyclopedia of Education* (2nd ed., Vol. 3, pp. 1643–1647). Oxford: Pergamon/Elsevier Science.

18
MACROSYSTEM

We come now to the most "distant" level of the ecosystem. It is also the most abstract of Bronfenbrenner's ecological concepts, and provides the greatest challenge to comprehension. Bronfenbrenner's challenge was to formulate a conception of the largest structure of the environment—culture—in a way that is consistent with, and an extension of, the smaller or "lower" levels of the environment. Those "lower" or nearer elements are the microsystem, mesosystem, and exosystem. Defining culture is always difficult, and defining it in ecological terms presents a problem. His solution to this problem is elegant: Culture, or the macrosystem, consists of the regularities or patterns within the microsystems and mesosystems typical of a particular group of people or region. In his original definition he describes it as "consistencies, in the form and content of lower-order systems" as well as the beliefs that go along with those consistencies (Definition 5, 1979, p. 26). In other words, if a group of people creates settings and relationships in particular ways, does things and plays roles in typical ways, and their ways of living differ from those of other groups of people, then these people participate in a culture or macrosystem. Such a group will also have preferred ways of explaining why they do things the way they do, and their beliefs about these will guide their behavior. The patterns of their ecosystem and their beliefs will distinguish their macrosystem from other macrosystems.

Later, Bronfenbrenner expanded his original definition to refer more specifically to the features of a macrosystem that might be more directly involved in creating differences in development in different macrosystems.

The macrosystem consists of the overarching pattern of micro-, meso-, and exosystems characteristic of a given culture or subculture, with particular reference to the belief systems, bodies of knowledge, material resources, customs, life-styles, opportunity structures, hazards, and life course options that are embedded in each of these broader systems. The macrosystem may be thought of as a societal blueprint for a particular culture or subculture.

(1994, pp. 1645ff.)

The "macro," or large, *sub*system of the ecosystem in which the person participates is the system that consists of the *similarities across settings within a larger environment*. We often refer to the larger environment as a society or culture. In develecological terms, if culture exists, it must be definable in terms of the ecosystem. It must have a meaning within the settings and microsystems we participate in. To Bronfenbrenner, culture exists as the consistency across settings, the ways that settings and microsystems are similar within a society or a community. Similarities across settings and microsystems, similarities in the way mesosystems are connected, and similarities in the nature of exosystems are often explained by or based on similarities across people in how they view the world. How we view the world, what we think is right, good, natural, necessary, etc., is a system of beliefs. *The components of the macrosystem* are the consistencies or similarities across settings and systems and the beliefs that are attached to those similarities. Beliefs and regularities are often manifested by the laws and public policies that determine the specific properties of exo-, meso-, and microsystems of everyday life and "steer the course of behavior and development" (Bronfenbrenner, 1979, p. 9). In Figure 18.1, the macrosystem is added to the graphic model.

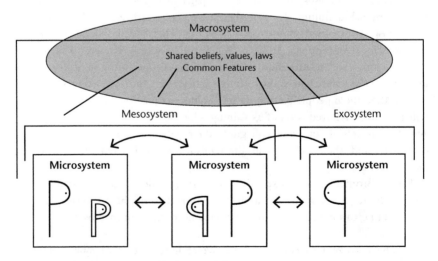

FIGURE 18.1   Macrosystem added to model

While many representations of Bronfenbrenner's framework suggest that the macrosystem is far removed from the developing person, this is misleading. In fact, *the developing person is constantly immersed in the macrosystem.* The settings, activities, roles, and relations the person participates in are part of the macrosystem. The macrosystem is the ways those settings, activities, roles, and relations *are similar to,* or consistent with, other settings, activities, roles, and relations. The macrosystem also includes *the reasons for those similarities,* the beliefs and ways of understanding the world that guide us in creating settings, activities, roles, and relations.

One way the macrosystem functions is by making it likely we will create new microsystems that are similar to our previous, familiar microsystems. We explain to ourselves our tendency to replicate our experience and institutions by saying "this is the way things *ought* to be," or "the way that *works best.*" But it is possible that we are just recreating what is familiar. It is possible that in fact we have never experienced or thought of any other way to do things. Cultures differ *if* and *because* people do things differently and have different beliefs about how they should be done. *Cultures differ* when they include *different versions* of the components of the ecosystem. Different macrosystems may have different roles, relationships, activities, settings, mesosystems, exosystems, and power settings, as well as different chronosystems.

What do we mean by consistencies across settings? As a familiar example, think about schools. Most westerners follow a trajectory of school settings, and most of those settings have similar microsystems: a teacher, students, perhaps a principal or headmaster, a curriculum, a school calendar, tests, grades, co-curricular activities, etc. We can move from community to community and expect to find schools, and expect that they will be familiar. *Those similarities (along with the rationales for them)* **are** *the macrosystem.* When we find a community that has a very different kind of education system, we experience it as foreign—representing a different macrosystem.

As another example, think about how groups of people make decisions in Western societies. We have a fundamental belief in representative democracy, including one vote for each person, and the majority rules. Such ideologies are incorporated in our constitutions and legal systems. We vote on a wide assortment of matters, beginning in preschool and continuing all our lives. We reject dictatorships. The fact that we enter most public situations expecting to vote on decisions represents our macrosystem. It is not a universal expectation; there are other, different, macrosystems.

The beliefs and assumptions of the macrosystem shape how we behave, how our microsystems operate, and what we experience as we grow up. The macrosystem, therefore, shapes the very nature of our view of the world we participate in and how we participate in it.

Multiple Macrosystems

Differences between cultures or subcultures exist, develecologically, as differences between typical microsystems and mesosystems. The differences are often connected to differences in beliefs or ideologies. One reason the notion of macrosystem is difficult to grasp is that it requires us to become aware of our beliefs and to see how they are connected to the patterns of our settings, microsystems, and mesosystems. We often are unaware of the fundamental beliefs we hold because we assume they represent the only way the world can be. Wars are fought because people do not understand that their particular macrosystem is one among many, not the only way to view the world. In Hypothesis 30 (1979, p. 213), Bronfenbrenner suggests that development is enhanced, that is, our view of the world is more valid, if we have the opportunity to experience *different* macrosystems, so we can see that there are differences, and that they are legitimate.

Macrosystems do not have neat borders; they overlap. A particular household may reflect two or more ethnic or religious traditions. It may have some consistencies with one culture, and other consistencies with a different culture. A community may encompass elements of several systems of belief. It then may be useful to think of the macrosystem of that household or that community as being mixed, or blended. In other cases, a household setting may be intensely congruent with other settings from the same cultural tradition. A community may comprise only households in which everyone shares the same set of beliefs and traditions. Conflict arises, potentially, when people whose macrosystems are different engage in transactions with each other. Conflict may arise between people when their macrosystem is in the process of change.

A consistent macrosystem may make development relatively easy, as roles, and activities and relationships are predictable and congruent across settings and across time. A blended or changing macrosystem may demand more complex skills and understanding if one is to develop competence. Hypothesis 30 reflects Bronfenbrenner's assumption that the modern multicultural world requires transactions with people whose traditions and beliefs and experiences will be quite different from one's own. Competence in a multicultural ecosystem is developed by engagement in settings, activities, and relationships that represent that diversity.

Macrosystem and Development

We are used to saying when something happens, or when a person develops in a particular way, that it happened, or the person is that way, because of culture, or societal influences. In develecology, it is necessary to explain culture or societal influence in a way that is integrated with the rest of the concepts of the ecological perspective. Thus, it must be represented in terms of activities, roles, relations, settings, microsystems, mesosystems, and the rest. Culture does not exist as a separate concept, apart from the details of the ecosystem. By referring to culture as the macrosystem and defining it as he does, Bronfenbrenner brings the ideas behind the notion of culture into the ecological framework he constructs. The idea that culture exists at the level of the ecosystem as similarities across roles, or activities, or relations, or settings, and so forth—elements of the ecosystem that may differ quite widely in different places—helps us understand how cultures, or macrosystems, influence development.

The macrosystem is not *causing* the development. Rather, the macrosystem is a feature of the context in which the development is happening. Development happens because a person engages in proximal processes in the relationships, settings, and systems available in the ecosystem. The person understands and becomes competent in the ecosystem in which experience occurs; the ecosystem shapes the development, but does not cause it. If ecosystems are similar, that is, they represent the same macrosystem, then it is likely the people who experience those ecosystems will develop similar views of the world, and skills and motivations. The people will thus be similar, and tend to perpetuate the macrosystem they are adapted to.

There is a potential misunderstanding when Bronfenbrenner writes that the macrosystem is the largest level of the ecosystem. Be clear that *the macrosystem does not include everything in the ecosystem*. Macrosystem refers to the patterns or consistencies across the other elements of the ecosystem. Be clear as well, that the macrosystem is a *sub*system within the ecosystem. The *eco*system is the largest, the whole, system we engage in and are part of. The other systems—micro, meso, exo, and macro—are all *subsystems* of the ecosystem.

A macrosystem facilitates development when it encourages development for all participants, when a person, the person's family, and their culture are valued. A macrosystem that supports development expresses beliefs and customs that encourage human development. If multiple macrosystems are present in an ecosystem, development is facilitated when the person has opportunities to experience and become familiar with all of them, not constrained to just one or hostile to the others. In other words, a macrosystem supports development when it encourages the construction of the most valid and differentiated understanding of the multiple cultures represented and the practice of skills that enable the person to relate effectively with all of them.

Remember: The macrosystem is not the community or where a person lives. It is the similarities or consistencies we see in how things are built, or how they are done, or how people relate to each other and what roles there are and how they are defined. The macrosystem includes the beliefs and values that people use to explain why they do things the way they do, or relate the way they do.

References

Bronfenbrenner, U. (1979). *The Ecology of Human Development: Experiments by Nature and Design.* Cambridge, MA: Harvard University Press.

Bronfenbrenner, U. (1994). Ecological models of human development. In T. Husen & T. N. Postlethwaite (Eds.), *International Encyclopedia of Education* (2nd ed., Vol. 3, pp. 1643–1647). Oxford: Pergamon/Elsevier Science.

19
CHRONOSYSTEM

Any attempt to explain development requires that we attend to the passage of time. Change can be defined only with reference to time. Many of Bronfenbrenner's definitions, propositions, and hypotheses refer to change. Yet his initial framework did not incorporate time as a specific element. Later, he added a specific reference to time in the notion of a "chronosystem."

> A **Chronosystem** encompasses change or consistency over time not only in the characteristics of the person but also of the environment in which that person lives (e.g., changes over the life course in family structure, socioeconomic status, employment, place of residence, or the degree of hecticness and ability in everyday life).
>
> *(1994, p. 1646)*

In general, the chronosystem represents the passage of time, as time affects the person, relationships, settings, mesosystems, the macrosystem, and all the other aspects of both the person and the ecosystem. All are moving through time. Ecosystems and their elements change for many reasons: time passes, history happens, the world changes. Change may occur quickly or slowly. Over time, the person adapts to changes that occur in herself, her settings, and all other components of the ecosystem. How rapidly changes happen may determine how easily the person adapts. In Figure 19.1, the chronosystem is added to complete the graphic model.

The chronosystem reflects technological and other changes in society that demand we develop new and different ways of understanding the environment and acting in it. A pertinent example can be found in Bronfenbrenner's discussion and hypotheses about intersetting communication in the section about links

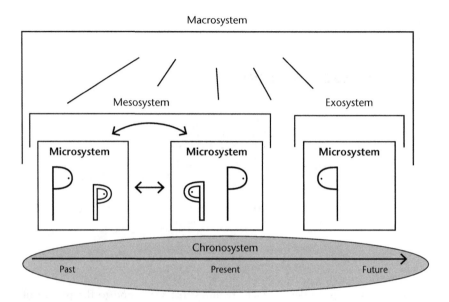

FIGURE 19.1 Chronosystem added to model

between settings. He was writing before the appearance of the multiple forms of digital communication and information that characterize life in the twenty-first century. So his hypotheses about communication didn't consider the possibilities of instant messaging, Skype, and the many forms of social media people use to communicate between settings now. Consider what the internet has done to the possibilities for creating intersetting knowledge. How much more quickly and easily do we access information about exosystem settings and incorporate information to create a more valid and differentiated view of our world?

Given the potentials of modern digital technology, we might even have to consider rethinking what constitutes participation in a setting. If we appear on Skype or video in a setting, and engage in two-way conversation electronically with others in the setting, are we participating in it, or do we have to physically be in it to participate? If the setting is a power setting, it may still be in our exosystem, but the chain of links may be very short if we can express our needs directly to the significant actors in the power setting by way of electronic media. We might argue that the digital revolution has increased the potential of every person to develop a more valid and differentiated view of the ecosystem. Does it also increase skills and motivation? Or *change* motivation and skills?

Rapid change in an ecosystem may strain our abilities to learn new ways of thinking, new ways of acting, of communicating. Failure to keep up with the changes in one's ecosystem may have a variety of consequences for the person. For instance, a person may adopt conservative rigidity, attempting to hang on to old ways and rejecting new. That strategy may be a source of conflict with other people in the system who embrace or perhaps embody the new. Examples may be found in intergenerational conflict in immigrant families or conflict among immigrants who embrace their new culture and blend in and those who do not.

Another possibility is that a person may experience anxiety and stress resulting from lack of understanding of events. Stress and incomprehension make a person vulnerable to physical stress disorders or emotional or mental illness. On the other hand, a person may come to love change and embrace whatever is new, without managing to understand the consequences of the changes or to appreciate the validity or value of previous states or systems.

The notion of chronosystem also applies to developmental research. In reading research, it is necessary to be aware of differences across historic time. For example, changes in the technology of the Neonatal Intensive Care Unit over the last 30 years have had major impact on the outcomes of premature birth. Studies of the development of babies who weighed 1,000 grams at birth in the 1970s don't compare to studies of 1,000-gram babies in the twenty-first century. The differences found between studies are not because premature babies have changed, but because their contexts are different. In studying developmental research, it may be very helpful to organize results according to the years when studies were conducted to begin to explain differences among them in results.

Another way the chronosystem may be involved in develecology is that people are aware of the passage of time, and may premise their behavior on assumptions about the future. An example of this was provided by a student who experienced interpersonal difficulty with a staff person in an internship setting. Analyzing the situation, the student determined how she could address the situation, and understood that if she were a co-worker, it would be necessary for her to take action. Since her internship was due to end in two weeks, however, she decided to put up with the other person's behavior. Developing a valid view of one's ecosystem and skills to manage in it may include understanding the implications of the passage of time.

In what sense is the chronosystem a system? What are its components and how are they related? How does change in one part of the chronosystem affect other parts?

Consider as one possibility that time passes differently in different settings. For example, technological change may have little impact on the roles and activities or on the mesosystem connections in an isolated small rural village. During the same period, roles, activities, and connections in an urban area may change drastically as technology becomes widely available. As differences between the two settings increase, they may represent progressively different macrosystems. Over the long term, the differences may affect the developmental trajectories likely for children growing up in each setting.

How might the chronosystem support a person's development in an ecosystem? If we think about changes in a macrosystem over time as examples of the chronosystem, we might find both general and specific illustrations. For a general illustration, it might be possible for a culture or subculture (macrosystem) to evolve or change over time so that it incorporates a more valid and differentiated view of people and their potential. It might provide more opportunities, roles, and activities for its members. The culture might reduce the barriers and hostility between settings, create better communication between settings, and offer more opportunities to participate in other cultures. Such changes across time might enhance development for everyone in the culture.

Chronosystem changes might also lead to better development for specific members or groups within the culture. Consider the changes in American culture involving extensions of Civil Rights. How have changes such as anti-discrimination laws, voting rights, affirmative action requirements, and desegregation changed the potential for development for African American children and adolescents over the last half-century? What settings have become open to children of color? What activities, relations, and roles are available that were not available 50 years ago? As another example, how has the development of people with disabilities been affected by passage of the Americans with Disabilities Act and the changing views of Americans toward people with disabilities?

In his work, Bronfenbrenner constantly examined how American society did and did not support the development of children and families. In his later years,

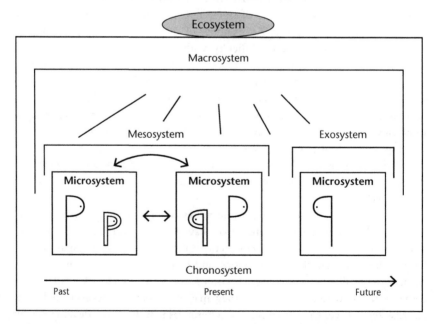

FIGURE 19.2   The completed structure of Bronfenbrenner's Ecological Systems Model

he became increasingly concerned that we were not supporting families and children. What changes in American society over the past 50 years might have caused him to become more concerned?

In a *developmentally facilitating ecosystem*, changes occur slowly enough that people can adapt to them with relative ease. The changes in the ecosystem improve opportunities and ability of each component to more effectively support development for more people.

Remember: The entire ecosystem is experiencing the chronosystem, or passing through time. All the components of the ecosystem change with the passage of time, including the Developing Person.

We have now completed the structure of Bronfenbrenner's Ecological Systems model. We will move on to examples Bronfenbrenner included in his 1979 book, and to possible ways we might explore using it.

Remember: The ecosystem contains all the subsystems we have discussed (see Figure 19.2).

References

Bronfenbrenner, U. (1979). *The Ecology of Human Development: Experiments by Nature and Design*. Cambridge, MA: Harvard University Press.

Bronfenbrenner, U. (1994). Ecological models of human development. In T. Husen & T. N. Postlethwaite (Eds.), *International Encyclopedia of Education* (2nd ed., Vol. 3, pp. 1643–1647). Oxford: Pergamon/Elsevier Science.

20
RESEARCH DESIGN

Bronfenbrenner was a developmental psychologist and researcher. Surveying the practice and products of research in the field, he grew deeply concerned that most developmental research does not address the ecosystem the subjects live in. Further, he saw that most studies of human development don't actually look at development—they don't measure changes in the subjects over time. He wrote:

> I have taken the position that development implies enduring changes that carry over to other places at other times. In the absence of evidence for such carry-over, the observed alteration in behavior may reflect only a short-lived adaptation to the immediate situation. For many of the ideas presented in this volume, it has been impossible to find an example in the research literature that met this important criterion. The great majority of studies in the field of human development do not in fact investigate changes in a person over any considerable time.
>
> *(1979, p. 14)*

Bronfenbrenner advocated for researchers to correct both shortcomings by conducting research that was both longitudinal and ecological. He provides a series of propositions to guide researchers to do studies that will help us understand the processes of development. In his book, *The Ecology of Human Development* (1979), he applied his ecological perspective to analyze and critique specific bodies of the research literature. He suggested specific ways the research was inadequate to answer the questions it addressed because it did not take an ecological perspective. He also identified research studies that much more effectively addressed the questions intended because they did use an ecological perspective. At the same time, he used his critiques and his examples to frame many of the hypotheses and propositions incorporated in his book and reiterated here.

Bronfenbrenner's very instructive examples in his book included a whole chapter devoted to the research laboratory as a setting for studying development. From that critique, he constructed definitions and propositions concerning research on development from an ecological perspective.

He begins by asserting that the world must be conceptualized in systems terms. Ecological research is complex and the way we go about it must reflect the complexity of the systems that shape development.

> In ecological research, the properties of the person and of the environment, the structure of environmental settings, and the processes taking place within and between them must be viewed as interdependent and analyzed in systems terms.
>
> *(PROPOSITION A, 1979, p. 41)*

He viewed the research setting itself as an ecological setting in the ecosystem, in which the researcher is a person, occupying a role and engaging in activities and relationships that will affect the subjects' behavior. In Proposition E (1979, p. 68) he identified the indirect effect on people by the presence of other people in the setting as a **second-order effect**, and insisted those effects must be studied as part of the analysis of research.

Ecological Validity

It may be helpful to remember that the subject in any research study is a developing person who occupies a unique ecosystem, has a particular understanding of the ecosystem, and individual skills and motivation for engaging with any setting. The subject has a developmental history that has led to the particular understanding, skills, and motivation. It is important for the researcher to attempt to be clear about any assumptions he or she is making about the subject, and to try to find out from the subject what the subject's understanding of the research and its setting might be.

Researchers always hope to demonstrate the validity of their research. If it isn't valid, why do it? Bronfenbrenner proposes that the several forms of validity researchers already consider (e.g., construct validity, content validity, face validity) should also include *ecological validity*, meaning that the researcher correctly understands how the subjects understand the research setting. To establish that the researcher's understanding is correct, the researcher has to attempt to study how the subject understands what's going on in the study. He defines ecological validity, and then offers two propositions about how to determine that a setting can produce ecologically valid research. He does not reject the idea that laboratories can produce ecologically valid research, but proposes conditions that must be met for ecologically valid research to be conducted in any setting.

> Ecological validity (in research) refers to the extent to which the environment experienced by the subjects in a scientific investigation has the properties it is supposed or assumed to have by the investigator.
>
> *(DEFINITION 8, 1979, p. 29)*

For research to be considered ecologically valid, two factors need to be studied. First, the researcher has to investigate and understand what the research experience means to the subject. Second, how the subject understands the experience has to correspond to the situation the researcher wants to generalize the findings to. Bronfenbrenner outlines these conditions as they apply to laboratory settings in Proposition G (1979, p. 121). Recognizing that much research is done outside the laboratory, and aware that some readers might consider any research done in a "natural" setting to be "ecologically valid," Bronfenbrenner crafted a more general form of Proposition G that applies to research in any setting, such as homes or schools or communities (Proposition G', 1979, p. 125).

Developmental Validity

Addressing his observation that much developmental research isn't really developmental, Bronfenbrenner suggests that before a researcher concludes development has happened, or that it has been influenced in some particular way, it is necessary to assess changes over both time and place. Only when such assessment has been made can the research be accepted as *developmentally valid*. Research that does not demonstrate that development has occurred may be quite useful, but only longitudinal research can tell us that development has happened. Cross-sectional research is about age differences, not about development.

> To demonstrate that human development has occurred, it is necessary to establish that a change produced in the person's conceptions and/or activities carries over to other settings and other times. Such demonstration is referred to as developmental validity.
>
> *(DEFINITION 9, 1979, p. 35)*

Bronfenbrenner then proceeds to define two specific types of experiments that are particularly important to the effort to understand develecology. If we are trying to understand the way development is influenced by an environment we view as a system, we can best acquire knowledge by comparing the influence of environments that differ in only one way. That allows us to learn about that one part of the system. Multiple versions of such an experiment focusing on different components of the ecosystem can lead toward understanding how the system functions as a whole. He defines an **ecological experiment** as an attempt to focus on the accommodation between the developing person and the ecosystem by altering a specific aspect of the ecosystem and assessing resulting differences in development (Definition 10, 1979, p. 36). Ecological experiments are designed to investigate specific connections between defined components of the ecosystem and defined aspects of development. As in other experiments, analyses include comparison of development before and after the alteration of the ecosystem or comparisons to development of subjects who did not experience the alteration.

Not all research involves carefully controlled ecological experimental manipulation. Bronfenbrenner considers the kind of experiment that happens when we tackle large issues, especially human or social problems, by changing a policy, or introducing a program, or attempting to promote social change. In these instances, he urges us to understand that we *are* engaging in research, that we should *assess the ecosystem* before we begin and continue assessing it through and after the activity, and that we should *simultaneously assess the development of persons* potentially affected by the changes we are making. In this way, we can learn how changes in one part of the ecosystem affect the other parts, and better understand which aspects of the alterations in which parts of the ecosystem are most important in promoting, and in hindering, development. He calls this sort of research a **transforming experiment**, because it involves changing the ecosystem in more or less permanent ways that may affect multiple aspects of the ecosystem (Definition 11, 1979, p. 41).

The sorts of experiments Bronfenbrenner refers to here include the introduction of Head Start, the creation of which he was involved in, or school reform, a constant current issue in the United States. Changes in welfare system benefits and requirements are another example. Introduction of new laws or public policies are also common. Such large changes often are introduced without prior assessment of the ecosystem in which they occur. Evaluations of them often focus on differences in specific limited measures of interest. Evaluations rarely include assessment of changes in the ecosystem or demonstration of developmental changes, and thus have neither ecological nor developmental validity.

Bronfenbrenner encourages us to study how social systems *inhibit* and *promote* development, especially of children and families, and to employ a develecological perspective to explain them. With this perspective, we can then design changes—transforming experiments—that are more likely to make them more effective in facilitating development. His approach also encourages us to do the complex research that makes it possible to conclude that our experiment does or does not work, and explain why, so we can design improvements. All of this may seem obvious to the intelligent person, but the reality is that social policy is often designed and implemented with little regard for understanding the human ecosystem and how it shapes development. Further, social policy changes often are implemented without provision for appropriate research to assess their effectiveness or to help define potential incremental improvements. While his examples are large-scale transformations, it is also possible to do small-scale transforming experiments, such as changing a policy within a school, or altering a family's microsystem by changing the approach to discipline. Regardless of scale, it is important to assess behavior or development prior to and after the transformation as well as to study how other aspects of the ecosystem respond to the changes.

In order to do research as Bronfenbrenner urges, we must first learn to see the world as made up of settings. We must learn to observe the activities people engage in, their complexity and diversity, observe the transactions people engage in, see the potentials, the risks and opportunities in settings, the relations among settings, the mesosystem and exosystem. When we have practiced and incorporated into our thinking a truly develecological view, then we can design, conduct, and interpret research as Bronfenbrenner urges those in the field to do. Beyond that, we will have a more differentiated and valid view of the world and the beginnings of skills to explore, maintain, and modify the ecosystem of which we are a part.

Before putting this chapter and topic aside, perhaps on the grounds that research is not of interest or use to you, let me point out that the concepts in this chapter may be pertinent to activities you might be involved in. Evaluation and assessment of programs and of proposals are a kind of research. You may be involved in trying to evaluate the effectiveness of a program. The concepts presented here may be applied to both the processes of evaluation and to programs themselves, especially in the areas of social services and education. It is important that as professionals providing services or education we view our work in systems terms, as indicated in Propositions A and E. It is important that we understand our programs as attempting to promote development and that we have a thorough understanding of the ecosystem in which we *and our clients or students* work and live, as suggested by Propositions G and G'. The concept of *Ecological Validity* applies not only to research, but also to programs. It seems clear that if a program is to be effective, the people conducting the program should have a valid understanding of the ecosystem and of the other people participating in the program. Thinking of evaluation of our efforts, when we claim that a program is successful, it would be useful for us to think of the *Developmental Validity* of our claims.

Reference

Bronfenbrenner, U. (1979). *The Ecology of Human Development: Experiments by Nature and Design*. Cambridge, MA: Harvard University Press.

21

BRONFENBRENNER'S EXAMPLES

In *The Ecology of Human Development*, Bronfenbrenner provides two examples of how to apply his framework, by interpreting two sets of research studies and offering hypotheses based on each. These provide models for how we might apply the framework to other topics of interest.

Orphanages and Hospitals

Bronfenbrenner's first example in his book is presented in Chapter 7, "Children's Institutions as Contexts of Human Development." He discusses the work of Rene Spitz (1945, 1946a, 1946b) which he writes, "represents an early prototype of an ecological model" (1979, p. 133). He concludes from Spitz's research that when young children are placed in institutional settings, their development is likely to be hindered. The ecological question is why does this happen, and under what circumstances. Such impairment has been attributed by some to maternal deprivation and by others to general impoverishment of environmental stimulation. From an extended analysis of the phenomenon and related research, Bronfenbrenner offers four hypotheses to guide research to help resolve the differences in interpretations, to determine the roles of experience in the ecosystem in producing the deleterious effects, and to test possible ecological interventions to avert the impairment. Among his hypotheses we find, in brief:

- Two ecological characteristics are likely to impede development, either separately or together. The first is if caregivers are unable to engage in a variety of joint activities with the child. The second is if the child's movement is restricted and there are few objects to play with (Hypothesis 15, 1979, p. 143).

- Impairment of development is most likely if the child is separated from its primary caregiver between six and 12 months, because that is when attachment is most intense (Hypothesis 16, 1979, p. 143).
- Impairment of development in institutions can be prevented or reversed if the setting provides opportunity for locomotion, caregivers engage in a variety of joint activities with the child, and a primary caregiver is available to foster attachment with the child (Hypothesis 17, 1979, p. 144).

His final hypothesis in this section addresses the importance of the age of the child in the transaction between the developing child and the potentially harmful institutional setting:

> The long-range deleterious effects of a physically and socially impoverished institutional environment decrease with the age of the child upon entry. The later the child is admitted to the institution, the greater the probability of recovery from any developmental disturbance after release. The more severe and enduring effects are most likely to occur among infants institutionalized during the first six months of life, before the child is capable of developing a strong emotional attachment to a parent or other caregiver.
>
> *(HYPOTHESIS 18, 1979, p. 150)*

Day Care and Preschool

Bronfenbrenner's second example focuses on another setting for children outside the home. His Chapter 8, "Day Care and Preschool as Contexts of Human Development," is devoted to a review and critique of research on the developmental effects of early childhood programs. This research was particularly important to Bronfenbrenner because of his role in creating the national Head Start program. In his critique of the literature, Bronfenbrenner cites the shortcomings of traditional research paradigms, which include failure to gather data on settings, outcome measures that are not ecologically valid, and focusing only on the child, rather than others who might be impacted by the program, such as parents. To encourage ecologically informed research, he provides six hypotheses employing elements of his framework. Again, briefly stated, he proposes:

- Child care will facilitate cognitive development if adults engage the child in task-oriented activities by questioning, responding, encouraging, etc., and the more often caregivers engage in such activities the greater will be the child's development (Hypothesis 21, 1979, p. 202).
- Microsystem features determine whether caregivers can facilitate a child's development. One key feature is the ratio of adults to children, which

affects how often the adults can engage each child in joint activities. The desirable ratio depends on the age of the children in the group (Hypothesis 22, 1979, p. 202).

The tendency for long-term care to lead to egocentric, aggressive, and antisocial behavior, especially among boys, is greater in macrosystems that value individualism and aggression for boys (Hypothesis 23, 1979, p. 203).

The molar activities a child participates in in early childhood settings influence which molar activities are initiated by the child at home, thus affecting development (Hypothesis 24, 1979, p. 203).

The types of roles and relations a child participates in in an early childhood setting influences how the child engages in relations and roles at home and in other settings (Hypothesis 25, 1979, p. 204).

Keep in mind that I have abbreviated these hypotheses. They have specific details that deserve consideration if you want to understand them better or apply them to specific situations or design research based on them.

The last hypothesis in this set focuses on the elements of the microsystem offered in an early childhood setting as they affect the potential to support development:

> The developmental potential of a day care or preschool setting depends on the extent to which supervising adults create and maintain opportunities for the involvement of children in a variety of progressively more complex molar activities and interpersonal structures that are commensurate with the child's evolving capacities and allow her sufficient balance of power to introduce innovations of her own.
>
> *(HYPOTHESIS 26, 1979, p. 204)*

Bronfenbrenner concludes his presentation of these hypotheses by pointing out that the hypotheses are generalizable to other settings where children participate, such as classrooms, playgrounds, and camps. This reminds us that he considered his framework a beginning point, not an end state. As a scientist, he expected that his concepts would be critiqued, refined, and clarified, and that as the framework was used in research, it would be expanded. He assumed ensuing generations of students, researchers, and teachers would apply the principles of his approach to new topics, and to generate sophisticated hypotheses specific to other issues. I share his hope that you will find his framework helpful and build on it to construct more sophisticated understanding and exploration of development in any and every context you engage in.

BOX 21.1

In the decades since Bronfenbrenner proposed these hypotheses, hundreds of studies have been published on the developmental effects of early childhood programs. How many of the studies have tried to test these hypotheses? How many studies could be interpreted as relevant to each of these hypotheses? How do they hold up in light of the available research?

BOX 21.2

Choose a topic in development or a problem you are interested in, review the relevant research, and analyze it using the develecological framework. Then formulate testable hypotheses about the ecological elements that contribute to the development or problem. See if you can formulate hypotheses about changes in elements of the ecosystem that might reduce the likelihood of the problem developing.

References

Bronfenbrenner, U. (1979). *The Ecology of Human Development: Experiments by Nature and Design.* Cambridge, MA: Harvard University Press.

Spitz, R. A. (1945). Hospitalism: An inquiry into the genesis of psychiatric conditions in early childhood. *Psychoanalytic Study of the Child,* 1, pp. 153–172.

Spitz, R. A. (1946a). Hospitalism: A follow-up report on investigation described in volume one 1, 1945. *Psychoanalytic Study of the Child,* 2, pp. 113–117.

Spitz, R. A. (1946b). Anaclitic depression: An inquiry into the genesis of psychiatric conditions in early childhood, II. *Psychoanalytic Study of the Child,* 2, pp. 313–342.

22

USING BRONFENBRENNER'S FRAMEWORK

Now that we have examined each of the major subsystems in Bronfenbrenner's framework, it is time to put them together, to integrate them into a complex, articulate language to describe the ecosystem and its parts and their relationship to human development. The systemic interconnections incorporated into the framework help keep us from focusing too narrowly on just one or some few of the elements in a person's life. Too often, we try to explain development or behavior as a function of some *one* relationship or event, when in reality, development is much more complex than that. Too often, we seize on a single action to try to change a complex situation, and are disappointed when simple solutions don't solve complex problems. Bronfenbrenner's framework reminds us of the complexity of life while at the same time it is a tool for conceptualizing the complexity. The framework can be applied to any person, any relationship, any setting, any community or society. It can guide us in analyzing any development, desirable or undesirable. We can use it to understand whether and how a particular ecosystem or subsystem supports development, or not. And we can apply it to guide us in making *changes* in relationships, activities, roles, settings, or communities to make them facilitate development more effectively. Bronfenbrenner's scheme provides a structure for *develecological analysis.* (Section 24 provides outlines for conducting such analysis.)

Develecological Analysis

To use Bronfenbrenner's scheme helpfully, we must learn to describe the ecosystem and all its elements clearly and precisely. The relationships among the elements must be characterized in consistent terms. The propositions and hypotheses then can be applied to the ecosystem as we have described it to determine how the elements and their relationships are helpful to development, and to *what* development. Finally, the implications of the hypotheses can be considered to create potential changes in the ecosystem that would alter its effects on development.

It is often helpful to sketch or outline the elements of the ecosystem and their relationships, beginning with the particular person whose development we wish to understand. What are the molar activities, roles, and relationships the person engages in? What settings does the person participate in regularly, and what are the characteristics of the microsystems in each of those settings? How are the settings linked? How supportive of each other are the microsystems in each setting? What exosystem settings affect or are affected by the person? How might each dyadic relationship or setting or microsystem or mesosystem relationship be altered to be more conducive to development? What activities might be added or changed to promote greater complexity and variety, and thus development?

Develecological analysis can begin with any part of the ecosystem. It can be applied to any behavior of interest, to any setting or its elements. It is particularly useful in understanding and designing ecological transitions between settings. For example, a develecological analysis helps us understand why some children have difficulty when they enter kindergarten, while others breeze through the change and thrive in school. The approach of analyzing and comparing past and new settings can help us anticipate the difficulties encountered by a couple who decide to live together, or the adjustments required by entering college and moving into a residence hall, or graduating from college and entering the working world.

Family transitions are particularly amenable to develecological analysis. Each transition in the family life cycle precipitates multiple changes in the ecosystem and has the potential to affect each family member's development. Marriage, moving into a new home, birth of a child, sending a child off to elementary school, the onset of puberty, divorce, remarriage, and all the other many changes that take place across life all affect the ecosystem. Most importantly, the particular ecosystem a person experiences can support, or not support, the development of the person as those changes occur.

For each level of the ecosystem, develecological analysis employing the propositions and hypotheses guides our inquiry. What are the characteristics of a healthy relationship? How do the activities of the relationship and the roles each person plays affect each person's development? What implications do changes in the relationship have for each person's development? How might specific changes in the dyadic relationship impact the two parties? How might third parties affect the dyad? Reciprocally, some family transitions are precipitated by change in the ecosystem.

How does the microsystem in a particular setting, such as a school, facilitate the development of the people who participate in it? How might the mesosystem of home, school, and parents' work settings more effectively foster children's development? How do extracurricular activities affect development? The range of situations and issues to which develecological analysis can be applied is as extensive as the ecosystem itself.

BOX 22.1

As you review Bronfenbrenner's hypotheses for each subsystem, see if you can create lists of conditions that support development, and that might not.

What experiences in what settings and ecosystems helped shape the person's particular understanding of the ecosystem, the world, and life? What experiences in those settings led to the skills and motives the person uses to explore, maintain, and modify the ecosystem?

The section of Exercises and Applications (Section 23) provides several types of examples I have used in classes to help students learn to use Bronfenbrenner's scheme. As with other aspects of development, a valid view of Bronfenbrenner's framework, and skill in applying it, come from the proximal processes of studying and practicing using it.

Understanding Development

Those of us who study development search for ways of thinking that put the myriad aspects of development into an organized framework. That is what Bronfenbrenner has done. He has distilled the essence of several different approaches into a single framework. His approach does not, and is not intended to, include every detail of development. It is, as he intended, a practical framework that puts the major features of development in context and defines their relationships. He has done this in a way that permits both analysis of individual development in context, and analysis of contexts according to their potentials for development.

Why use Bronfenbrenner? There are few, if any, alternative perspectives that focus on process and facilitation in a practical way.

Bronfenbrenner's scheme is comprehensive. It puts all people into the same framework. All development fits. One does not have to have a separate theory about development in poverty or theories of delinquency or drug abuse or other social problems. Bronfenbrenner assumes all people are following the same *general principles* of development, and all people are growing, learning, and experiencing in some context. Differences among individuals and differences among contexts can then be identified to explain differences that arise during the course of development. The framework directs our attention to elements of the environment that may be most helpful in explaining differences in the course of development experienced by or manifested by different people.

The honors student, the successful politician, the drug addict, and chronic thief are all following the same developmental principles. There are person-specific differences that may help in understanding their different experiences, motivations, and behaviors. And there are differences in settings, microsystems, ecosystem, risks, and opportunities to be analyzed to understand the development of their specific views of the world and their skills.

The framework is general enough to be powerful, open enough to permit incorporation of new discoveries. It respects individual differences and not only applies across situations and cultures, but *incorporates situations and cultures* into its analysis of the course of development. With the incorporation of the passage of time (the chronosystem), it accounts for differences that have historical origin.

It is a robust system with few assumptions. Physicists search for a "unifying theory" to tie together our understanding of the nature of the several forces in the universe and how they operate jointly. Bronfenbrenner provides such a unifying perspective for the study of human development.

And it is fundamentally useful. Applying a Bronfenbrennerian perspective provides a basis for predicting the effects of changes in settings or relations. The perspective permits and encourages hypotheses about ways to change environments to promote developments of specific sorts. It focuses us on particular key elements to understand the effects of changes. It suggests what to look for when we observe changes in behavior or differences between development in different situations.

Facilitating Development

All the activities and problems of human behavior involve change. Both developmental and ecological perspectives are necessary for comprehending problems, and for addressing improvements. Whether we are talking about adjustment, adaptation, learning, education, or rehabilitation, we are talking about development. When we consider social services, crime, poverty, intimate partner violence, child abuse, nurturing babies at risk, or nurturing gifted and talented children, we are talking about development. We need to be able to conceptualize the transactions between the person and the environment if we hope to change the environment so as to support development and reduce the incidence of the problems. We need to keep in mind that people are always adapting to and trying to understand the relations, roles, and activities of the ecosystems they inhabit.

Develecology provides a framework for analyzing any person's development, any setting, any activity or enterprise, any problem or situation, any policy. Develecology provides a framework for consideration of changes in the ecosystem to facilitate development more effectively. How might a classroom and the ecosystem in which it exists be changed to make it more supportive of a particular child? Or to make it better promote collaborative work?

Conversely, develecology provides a framework for consideration of changes that would make a setting *less* helpful to an individual's development. It is important to be able to describe how an ecosystem functions and why it functions less well than intended. If we can describe how to make an ecosystem less supportive of development, we may be able to understand why some efforts to combat problems actually make them worse. Some developments are undesirable. If the complex molar activity being supported in an ecosystem is drug abuse, then it is reasonable to try to change the system so it is less supportive of that form of development. Of course, at the same time one might want to consider changes that would support alternative, more desirable trajectories.

Develecological Values

Earlier, in Section 16, I suggested that developmental outcomes could be explained without judgment. Does that mean that develecology leaves us without a means to determine right from wrong or what is good or bad development? I said there that judgment was a macrosystem issue, and that implies that belief or cultural standards of morality would guide such considerations. Let me suggest here, that it might be possible to apply Bronfenbrenner's principles to determine whether a particular developmental trajectory or outcome is good or bad, making such considerations consistent with the rest of his ecological approach.

My first thought is that specific developmental paths might be evaluated on the basis of whether and how they affect the person's future development and participation in the ecosystem. Does engaging in a particular molar activity limit the potential to engage in other activities or to increase the complexity and variety of activities the person can engage in? Does the activity prevent the formation of developmental dyads? Does it restrict opportunities to enter other settings that might promote development, or prevent the formation of developmental trajectories? Do the view of the world or the abilities of the person hinder development by interfering with successful adaptation to new settings? Do the effects of the activity or the microsystems in which it occurs endanger biological development, health, or access to supportive resources? Might these develecological effects of the prior development serve as the basis for deeming it *ecologically undesirable*?

A second approach to evaluating the desirability of a person's development might be to consider the impact of the person's behavior on the ability of other people in the ecosystem to develop. If the behavior impinges on the potential development of other persons, then we might consider it undesirable. I welcome further reflection on the issue of assessing the relative value of any development, within the framework of develecology.

Develecology is useful in any area of human endeavor because it is helpful to understand the proximal processes in which all humans engage and the distal processes that might affect them. No development, no change in the person or the environment can be assumed to have no impact; we all live in complex systems. Our very development and our progress as individuals and societies and as a species depend upon constructing a more differentiated and valid view of the systems we participate in.

Human issues and social problems are not simple. Issues, problems, conflicts, and successes all have developmental histories, like people. Social and interpersonal problems rarely have simple causes, and even more rarely do they have simple solutions.

Broader Uses and Extensions

In this introduction to Bronfenbrenner's framework, we have focused on develecological analysis applied to individuals. We have emphasized learning to understand the ecosystem from the perspective of a single developing individual. In this approach, the developing person has one mesosystem, and that mesosystem has one primary link among all its settings. That link is the developing person. After one has learned to apply the develecological approach consistently to a single person's ecosystem, the next step is to use the framework to consider the shared and overlapping ecosystems of a couple, and more complexly, of an entire family.

Keeping in mind that each person has a uniquely defined ecosystem, we can then combine them to characterize where they overlap. A couple, for example may share many settings, but also occupy some settings individually. We may refer to the shared settings as the "couple mesosystem." Similarly, a couple may share a macrosystem, having come from the same or very similar macrosystem. Their couple relationship may be quite different from the relationship of a second couple who come from very different macrosystems. As experience in two different macrosystems may be expected to lead to different conceptions of the ecosystem, the second couple may have more differences in their views of the world, with potential implications for couple conflict. What skills might it take for them to maintain reciprocity and a balance of power? Could we expect the people in the second couple to have more extended, differentiated and valid views of the ecosystem, as a result of their experiences with each other?

The analysis of the ecosystem occupied by a family—a larger group of developing individuals—requires even greater complexity. Family systems theory, research, and therapy typically emphasize the system of relationships, roles, and activities *within* the family, but the family also participates in a larger ecosystem including the community. A develecological analysis that includes the combined mesosystems and exosystems of the family members, as well as their macrosystem and chronosystem, provides a rich and potentially very useful understanding of their strengths and their problems or challenges.

Beyond the family, develecological analysis can be applied to a generalized ecosystem, such as a community. This next level of analysis combines the overlapping individual ecosystems of the members of the larger group to conceptualize the larger ecosystem and how it supports development of the people who participate in it. This more abstract use of the framework can be applied to *any social group*—a neighborhood, a community, employees of an organization, such as a corporation, staff, and clients of a social service agency, a baseball team, or any other imaginable group. Such an analysis can be applied to understand why some members of a group do not develop well, compared to others. The hypotheses Bronfenbrenner offered then can be used to design changes to the ecosystem under study to improve its potential for fostering development.

Develecological analysis can form the basis for evaluation of the effectiveness of an agency or program whose mission includes supporting the development of participants. While most social service programs don't say specifically they are trying to promote development, in reality that is precisely what they are trying to do. An assessment that looks at the ecosystem of the program and its participants offers a valuable perspective and may identify potential changes to the program that would make its role and activities in the ecosystem of the client participants more likely to promote their development. I have been assigning my students to conduct such analyses of families, groups, agencies, and programs for many years, and have been constantly impressed by the depth and power develecology brings to understanding how each functions. Develecological analysis is a powerful tool for understanding how people, families, and organizations work, why they sometimes don't, and how they might be improved.

Employing the framework to construct a develecological perspective of a group of the sort suggested requires examining the settings specific to the group, as well as how the ecosystems of individual members overlap with and relate to the group settings. The develecologist then asks questions about the ways the group ecosystem supports the development of members, both individuals and subgroups. What activities, roles, and relationships are open to which participants? Where are the power settings, and who do they favor? Which policies or practices support whose development? How do the individual private settings of members and the group settings relate to and support each other and their constituent microsystems, reciprocally? What developmental trajectories are encouraged in the group ecosystem? Such applications of the framework were very important to Bronfenbrenner as he developed his perspective. In his research and in his public life, he advocated strongly for the necessity and the potential benefits of applying the principles of development and of ecology to understand and address human and social problems.

Bronfenbrenner advocated strongly for a related use of his perspective when he urged us to apply it to identify the impact proposed social policies or programs might have on children and families. He suggested that whenever a legislative body such as Congress considered a change to laws governing social programs, they should prepare a family impact assessment of the proposed changes. He wanted social policy to be guided by the goal of increasing the potential for development for all citizens, and to focus on removing barriers to development that are created in some ecosystems. This approach has not been widely adopted in our social systems, but could be, if more people understood the principles of develecology and recognized the central role of human development in the quality of life in society.

Cautions and Next Steps

For a balanced (and more valid) view, we must also consider what Bronfenbrenner's approach is not useful for. I have said that develecology helps explain development in context. It is more precise to say it provides a *framework* for explaining development in context. It is a framework into which we must place sophisticated understanding of biological processes, gene expression, individual differences, cognitive processes, interpersonal relations, group processes, and so forth. It organizes those, but cannot substitute for them. The student of development is obligated to continue to learn concepts, theories, and empirical relationships, or the framework has nothing to organize. Understanding development well requires us to become develecologists, able to integrate the developmental and the ecological perspectives and processes. We must learn to conceptualize changes in both the person and the environment and how they transact over time.

Bronfenbrenner's ecological framework is not by itself a theory of human development. He provided a definition of human development that is consistent with an ecological perspective. He drew our attention to the reality that most theory and research did not adequately address the role of the environment or the person's transactions with the environment. He laid out a systematic framework for understanding how the environment shapes development and encouraged us to observe and describe the proximal processes and the transactions of the person in and with the environment. He provided us a very powerful tool for developing our own more extended, differentiated, and valid view of our ecosystems and of our work. His framework provides a challenge to any theory of development, and guides us in assessing the validity of theory and research in the field. Theories and research are still necessary.

Bronfenbrenner's approach assumes a generally constructivist theory of development, an active human organism, and the importance of relationships, but in his ecology of human development, he is not much more specific about the processes involved. For those, we must dig deeper into developmental theory and research, including Bronfenbrenner's later work.

Bronfenbrenner's exploration of develecology led him to focus on the relation between the person and environment, and more specifically on the role of biological processes in that relation. This is what is commonly referred to as the relationship between "Nature and Nurture." Working with his colleague Stephen Ceci, they elaborated on the role of the person's experience in the process of gene expression. As they published critiques of gene/environment analyses characteristic of research in the 1980s and 1990s, their work (Bronfenbrenner & Ceci, 1993, 1994a, 1994b) influenced the development of more sophisticated views of what we mean by "nurture" in understanding the transactional roles of biology and experience in development. In this work, he explored and refined his conceptualization of his "bioecological" perspective on development.

Now that you understand the basics of the ecosystem, you are prepared to pursue the elaborations Bronfenbrenner made toward a fuller representation of the complex nature of human development in context. Reading his major elaborations in chronological order will support an appreciation for the evolution of his thinking and his contribution to our field. I suggest these as core reading, in this order: Bronfenbrenner (1992, 1995a, 1995b) and Bronfenbrenner and Morris (2000). A wider representation of his work is collected in *Making Human Beings Human* (2005), writings selected and edited by Bronfenbrenner.

References

Bronfenbrenner, U. (1979). *The Ecology of Human Development: Experiments by Nature and Design*. Cambridge, MA: Harvard University Press.

Bronfenbrenner, U. (1992). Ecological systems theory. In R. Vasta (Ed.), *Annals of Child Development, Vol. 6, Six Theories of Child Development: Revised Formulations and Current Issues* (pp. 187–249). London: Jessica Kingsley.

Bronfenbrenner, U. (1995a). The bioecological model from a life course perspective: Reflections of a participant observer. In P. Moen, G. H. Elder, Jr., & K. Luscher (Eds.), *Examining Lives in Context: Perspectives on the Ecology of Human Development* (pp. 599–618). Washington, DC: American Psychological Association.

Bronfenbrenner, U. (1995b). Developmental ecology through space and time: A future perspective. In P. Moen, G. H. Elder, Jr., & K. Luscher (Eds.), *Examining Lives in Context: Perspectives on the Ecology of Human Development* (pp. 619–647). Washington, DC: American Psychological Association.

Bronfenbrenner, U. Ed. (2005). *Making Human Beings Human: Bioecological Perspectives on Human Development*. Thousand Oaks, CA: Sage.

Bronfenbrenner, U. & Ceci, S. J. (1993). Heredity, environment, and the question "How?" A new theoretical perspective for the 1990's. In R. Plomin & G. E. McClern (Eds.), *Nature, Nurture, and Psychology* (pp. 313–323). Washington, DC: American Psychological Association.

Bronfenbrenner, U. & Ceci, S. J. (1994a). Nature-nurture reconceptualized: A bioecological model. *Psychological Review*, 101, 568–586.

Bronfenbrenner, U. & Ceci, S. J. (1994b). Toward a more developmental behavioral genetics. *Social Development*, 3, 64–65.

Bronfenbrenner, U. & Morris, P. A. (2000). The ecology of developmental processes. In R. Lerner (Series Ed.) & W. Damon (Vol. Ed.), *Handbook of Child Psychology: Vol. 1. Theory* (5th ed., pp. 993–1028). New York: Wiley.

23

EXERCISES AND APPLICATIONS

These are some *activities* that may help you study and understand develecological principles.

Understanding Bronfenbrenner's Definition of Human Development

1   Briefly describe an example of a period in your life when you developed. What was your experience? Explain how you know you developed.

2   Describe your conception, or understanding, of the ecological environment at the beginning and then after your developmental experience. The difference that emerged will be the focus of the remaining entries.

3   Describe the ways your conception of the environment became more extended, more differentiated, and more valid as you went through this developmental experience.

4   Identify in what ways you became more motivated and more able to engage in activities that revealed the properties of the environment.

5   Identify in what ways you became more motivated and more able to engage in activities that sustained the environment or restructured it at levels of similar or greater complexity in form and content.

Basic Concepts

1   Describe two very important molar activities you engage in. Explain how these two activities satisfy the criteria in Bronfenbrenner's definition of molar activity.

2   Describe two important dyads you participate in with different people.

Then explain for each the properties of affect, power, and reciprocity the relations exhibit.

3 Describe one important setting in your ecosystem. Then describe the microsystem that exists in it.

4 Pick three important settings in your mesosystem. Describe the links between each pair of settings. How do the relationships in Hypotheses 28, 34, 35, 36, 38, and 40 apply to these settings in your mesosystem?

5 a Describe an important event or series of related events in your life.

  b What influence did the experiences described have on your life/ development?

  c Translate your description into Bronfenbrennerian terms. See if you can find within your description illustrations of each of these:

- an ecological transition
- a molar activity
- a change in developmental status
- a change in a dyad
- a change in a relation
- a change in a role
- support for propositions C or F
- a change in a mesosystem
- support for five of the hypotheses.

Elaborate on the illustrations you find, to explain them. If you don't find illustrations, try choosing a different event to analyze.

Develecological Principles

Sort out from Bronfenbrenner's framework a clear statement of your understanding of what conditions of the ecosystem are most supportive of human development. What are the features of an ecosystem that will facilitate development? This will require that you study the hypotheses pertinent to each element of the system and try to abstract the important features and then synthesize them into a set of principles that express how an ideal ecosystem would operate.

Develecological Parenting

From a develecological perspective, parents have the responsibility to manage a child's participation in the ecosystem, to manage the ecosystem the child participates in, and to help the child develop a valid and differentiated view of the ecosystem and the skills to operate effectively within it.

If you accepted and conscientiously applied Bronfenbrenner's propositions and hypotheses, how would you raise children? What would you do? How would you relate? What actions would you take to create and maintain a developmentally facilitating microsystem for the children you were raising? What would you do to make their mesosystem as supportive of their development as possible? How would you make sure that exosystem settings did as much as possible to support your child's development? What would you do to help the child understand and function well in the macrosystem you participate in? What could you do to help prepare the child to adapt easily to new ecosystems it might encounter in the future?

Develecological Rules for Raising Children

Drawing on your understanding of the role of the family setting and its context in children's development, write a set of rules for raising children. Explain the significance of each rule and support each rule with your understanding of Bronfenbrenner's scheme. Be specific and clear and support your rules. It may help to give an example of what one would do in following each rule.

Eco-Autobiography, Version 1

Create a personal eco-autobiography—an interpretation of your own development and life in ecological terms. The goal is to create a narrative that explains how your participation in the ecosystem has shaped your development—your understanding of the world, your skills and motivation, your values, your relationships, and your goals. The following steps may be useful.

1   Make a list of the important concepts, definitions, propositions, and hypotheses in Bronfenbrenner's scheme. As you read about his framework, free associate to possible examples in your own life. If you do this as an ongoing journal (perhaps on your word processor), you may find your understanding growing, and your eco-autobiography evolving.
2   Pick a significant episode in your life—summer camp, coming to college, your parents' divorce or remarriage, your first real job, etc.—and write a narrative account of it. Try to explain what effect this episode had on your development, and why. Then go back and connect Bronfenbrenner's concepts to your story. Find an example of an ecological transition, for example. Figure out which of his hypotheses apply to your experience. You will be translating your experience into his concepts, and that may serve as the foundation for your eco-autobiography.
3   Pick a place where you regularly spend time. Describe its physical characteristics. What activities are possible in that place? What activities are likely to happen? What activities cannot happen there? What relationships exist in that place? How are they shaped by the physical space and the activities that happen in it? What roles can people take on in that space? How do those roles relate to the types of relationships people experience in the space? Can

you describe the *pattern* of all three elements—activities, relationships, and roles—that happen in that space in a typical day when you are present?

4   Make a list of the most important activities you engage in. Then, for a couple of them, try to describe how they developed. When did you start doing them, how have they changed over time? Why have they changed? What settings were important to doing them? Do they illustrate a developmental trajectory?

5   Draw a representation of your current mesosystem, including the ways different settings are linked to each other.

6   Describe the development of a relationship that is or has been significant to you. How did it begin? What did you do together? How did the relationship change over time, and why? How would you characterize the affect, power, and reciprocity in the relationship? How did each component change over time? How did changes affect your satisfaction with the relationship?

7   Write a brief statement including five beliefs that are very important to you. How did those beliefs come to be part of your view of the world? Who else shares those beliefs? Who does not share those beliefs with you?

Eco-Autobiography, Version 2

Create an eco-autobiography that focuses on your current development and the social ecosystem that has shaped your development.

1   What is your current view of the ecosystem you live in? What skills and motivation do you have for exploring, maintaining, and extending your ecosystem? What experiences have shaped your view, your skills, and your motivation? What is your current Developmental Status, according to the complexity and variety of the molar activities you engage in when you are on your own?

2   What developmental trajectories are you on currently? What do they suggest about your future development?

3   What settings, relationships, activities, and roles are prominent in your life? How do they contribute to your development? What changes could you make in each that might facilitate your development more?

4   Thinking of the important settings in your past and current ecosystems, what settings were unique to you, and how did they affect your development? What settings were absent from your ecosystem that might have contributed to your development had they been present?

24

ECO-ANALYSIS

Eco-analysis is the application of develecological concepts to interpret a person's development, a situation, a setting, an activity, a family, a social agency, an institution, a policy, or a problem. The point is to interpret the topic of the analysis in ecological and developmental terms. The analysis should lead to a more differentiated, extended, and valid view of the object of your analysis. Once you have an eco-analysis of the current situation, you may be able to apply Bronfenbrenner's hypotheses to suggest ways to change the ecosystem so that it might better support development.

Beginning Eco-Analysis

The purpose of eco-analysis is to translate the object of the analysis into ecological terms, to develop a view of the ecosystem in which the topic exists. List the elements of the ecosystem as we have spelled them out in this book, and then identify how they are represented in the ecosystem you are analyzing. The list would include:

The people involved, and especially the developing people
The settings (activities, roles, and relations possible and appropriate in it)
Roles (variety, applicable to other settings)
Activities (molar, complex, assigned or chosen)
Relations (affect, power, reciprocity)
The microsystems in important settings (patterns)
Links and relations between settings
The mesosystems of the people involved
Important exosystem settings

The macrosystem consistencies relevant to the topic
Developmental trajectories of the people involved
Ecological transitions experienced by the people
Chronosystem changes affecting the topic

Once you have constructed a clear understanding of the ecosystem involved, you can begin to consider the hypotheses that suggest what features of an ecosystem are helpful to development. Where in the ecosystem do you detect conditions that support development? *What* development is being supported? Where do see that the conditions of the ecosystem might be altered to better support development?

Advanced Develecological Analysis

A more complex *develecological* analysis or investigation adds to the ecological analysis more deliberate and sophisticated attention to the current and potential development of the parties involved. Remember that Bronfenbrenner defines development as the process of acquiring a more extended, differentiated, and valid view of the ecosystem and the skills and motivation to transact with the ecosystem in ways that maintain or improve it. Develecological analysis starts with describing the elements of the ecosystem as outlined in the preceding section, and then attempts to investigate how the people of interest view the ecosystem and what skills and motivation they have for dealing with it. In develecological analysis, we are trying to understand the ecosystem features that have shaped the person's understanding and skills, and how the understanding and skills are being used by the person to adapt to and be competent in the current ecosystem. We hope to understand the transactions the person is having with the ecosystem.

When we acquire our own differentiated and valid view of the transactions our subject has with the ecosystem, then we can begin to hypothesize about specific changes in the ecosystem that might support further development for the person. Again, we use our list of ecosystem elements, along with our understanding of the conditions of the ecosystem that support development, to define potential changes that might alter the transactions the person engages in. Possibilities might include, for example:

Could we explain to the person in more detail how the microsystem in a setting functions, and what the person might do to adapt more effectively?

Could a specific relation the person participates in be changed to be more like a developmental dyad?

Could activities be made more complex?

Could the person be engaged in practice of skills that will be helpful to more effective adaptation in the setting?

Could the affect in relations become more positive?

Could the person be granted more power in relations?

Could the other person in a relation encourage more reciprocity?

Could the roles expected and available to the person be changed, expanded, or new ones added?

Could the microsystem pattern be made more comfortable for the person?

Could the mesosystem be expanded to provide for participation in more diverse settings, thus perhaps differentiating and extending the person's view of the ecosystem?

Could the links and relations between settings in the mesosystem become more favorable to the person's development?

Could people in settings in the exosystem be helped to acquire a more valid view of the person and the person's ecosystem and how it might be supported?

Could current or potential developmental trajectories be strengthened, or, if a current developmental trajectory is considered to be undesirable, could the activities and settings involved in the trajectory be bent toward a more positive direction?

These are only some of the possible modifications that could be made using Bronfenbrenner's hypotheses. Bronfenbrenner's framework and hypotheses offer a wide array of ways an ecosystem could be improved to support development. As well, they can help us identify corresponding barriers to development and adaptation. There are no limits to the potential uses of a develecological analysis. We are limited only by our imaginations.

Example: Develecological Analysis of a Problem

Understanding a problem in develecological terms is a challenge, but can lead to a more sophisticated and valid view of the situation. The resulting develecological view may suggest approaches to dealing with the problem that are likely to be more ecologically sound and ultimately effective.

For the first step, focus on the problem as you understand it. Don't attempt to incorporate proposed solutions to the problem. Solutions should be proposed only after you have a thorough ecological understanding of the problem. As you later develop potential solutions, your ecological understanding may change, to become more valid, but for now, focus only on your understanding of the problem.

Use Bronfenbrennerian concepts to frame your topic and place the issue or problem in the ecosystem by answering the following questions. Not all of them will have definitive answers, but you should be able to explain why they don't.

1   What is the problem?
2   What people are involved
3   What settings are involved?
4   How are those settings connected? What connections are *not* present?
5   What is the microsystem in each setting?
6   How does the problem relate to the microsystem patterns?
7   What molar activities are involved in the creation and maintenance of the problem? How complex are they? Are they inconsistent?
8   What roles contribute to the creation and maintenance of the problem?
9   What relationships are part of the problem or affected by it?
10 Whose development *is affected by* the problem? Use Bronfenbrenner's definition of development. Specify the view of the world and the skills that are affected.
11 Whose development or incomplete development *contributes to the problem*? (If you later create a proposal to address the problem, it will need to detail how you will facilitate their development in desired directions.)
12 How does the mesosystem support the creation or maintenance of the problem? Is a developmental trajectory involved? Specify the settings and activities that compose the trajectory.
13 What exosystem settings are involved in the problem, and how do they support the creation or maintenance of the problem?
14 How does the macrosystem support the creation or maintenance of the problem? Specify the consistencies across settings and the beliefs that underlie them.

It may be useful to try to draw the ecosystem in which the problem exists.

When you are finished, try to describe the ideal world: What would the ecosystem be like *without* the problem?

If you develop a proposal or solution to the problem, specify what new settings, roles, activities, mesosystem, connections, etc. will result from the activities you propose.

Develop two or three proposals and compare their develecological potentials.

Develecological Analysis of a Policy or Program

As a variation, try a develecological analysis of a proposed or current social policy or program to understand how it will or does affect the ecosystems of the people it proposes to help. How will the ecosystem operate to resist the program? How could the ecosystem be engaged more productively? How could the program be improved, using develecological principles?

25

DEVELECOLOGY 001

Bronfenbrenner Made Plain

This is my attempt to provide a simple translation of Bronfenbrenner's framework, in plain English. It is a rough approximation, and not intended to substitute for the original, or for my interpretation in the body of this book. It may be useful as a reminder, and as a way of constructing a more familiar understanding of the central assumptions of Bronfenbrenner's approach.

People develop and adapt to their environment.

Development happens in and is shaped by the specific features of the ecosystem we participate in.

Development means acquiring a more valid and differentiated view of the world we live in and the skills and motivation to maintain it, adapt to it, and restructure it to make it better meet our needs.

People participate in activities, relations (or dyads), and roles.

Activities vary in complexity.

In development, activities become more complex, more important, and more intrinsically motivating.

Activities that promote development have the potential to become more complex.

Roles are defined by particular activities and relations and are a way we organize experience and expectations.

People in specific roles engage in specific activities and relate to others in typical ways. Activities and relationships in some roles are specifically prescribed, while others are more flexible and varied.

Roles are typically transactional, that is, they involve two or more complementary roles, with defined transactions between them. Such pairs of roles include parent and child, husband and wife, student and teacher, for example.

Being around people who occupy a variety of roles is good for development, because it facilitates our understanding of the world.

Having the opportunity to occupy a variety of roles is good for development, because it improves understanding of the roles and their activities and relations, and allows us to practice skills involved in those roles.

Relations, or what happens between the people in dyads can be described according to their characteristics, including:

- *affect*—the feelings involved;
- *reciprocity*—the give and take of the transaction; and
- *power*—who influences whom and directs the activities of the dyad.

Relations are most attractive or engaging when they involve positive affect, high reciprocity, and relatively equal power.

Dyads are of several types, depending on their functions:

- Observational—one person watches the other.
- Joint Activity—two people engage in an activity together.
- Primary—both people think about each other, even when apart.
- Developmental—one person is more developed than the other, they engage in activities together, reciprocity gradually increases, power becomes more balanced, and both share positive affect.

These types are not mutually exclusive: a particular dyad can be both primary and developmental, for example.

Relations are *transactional*. What happens between two people is a transaction. Both people are changed by participating in their relationship.

Participation in a variety of activities in dyads with a variety of people promotes development.

Observational dyads tend to become joint activity dyads, which tend over time to become primary dyads.

As people participate in several different dyads, the degrees to which these dyads support each other, are compatible with each other, or are in conflict with each other, become important.

In development, engaging in activities and transactions with others are "*proximal processes*" and are experiences from which people construct understanding and skill. This is a *constructivist viewpoint* of development.

A *setting* is a physical place where people can engage in face-to-face contact with each other.

Each setting has a unique pattern of roles, relations, and activities, or *microsystem* within it. The physical characteristics determine what that pattern can be.

People *adapt* to the pattern in each setting. Adaptation is an active, but not necessarily conscious, process of understanding the setting and how its microsystem operates. The participants in the microsystem do the activities, engage in the relations, and carry out the roles, and these are likely to become part of the person's understanding and expectations for that part of the ecosystem.

Microsystem patterns can be characterized as rigid, chaotic, organized, flexible, stable, changing, etc.

Change in any aspect of a microsystem requires adaptation, and potentially evolution of a new pattern.

Change in a role or setting is called an *"ecological transition"* for the person.

In the course of development people become able to make transitions more easily, learning to move through our regular settings smoothly, and in and out of roles.

Maturity, or *developmental status*, is indicated in several ways:

- How well we understand the ecosystem and how skilled we are at functioning in it, maintaining it, and modifying it to better promote our development.
- The variety and complexity of the activities we engage in when we're choosing them on our own.
- The variety and complexity of the roles we occupy.
- The number and variety of relationships we engage in with positive affect, high reciprocity, and equal power.
- Our skill at engaging in developmental dyads as the more developed person.
- Our ability to adapt to ecological transitions.

People participate in more than one setting. Settings are different from each other, each having a unique microsystem determined by the physical characteristics of the settings, the particular roles incorporated in it, the activities engaged in by the people in it, and the relations among those participants. The number and variety of the settings we engage in typically increase as we develop.

Each person has one unique *ecosystem*, defined from the perspective of that particular person.

Each person participates in a number of microsystems, one in each setting.

The settings a person engages in are related to each other. The relations among those settings make up the one *mesosystem* each person has.

That mesosystem of settings also relates to other settings the person doesn't enter. Those settings and their relations to the mesosystem are referred to as the *exosystem*.

To the extent that roles, activities, settings, microsystems, and mesosystems are similar to each other across a group of people, there is a *macrosystem*. The macrosystem, or the consistencies across settings, roles, etc. is what we call culture.

The mesosystem is characterized by how the settings in it relate to each other. This includes how they are linked.

The *primary link* among settings is the person who moves in and out of them, connecting them and thus defining which settings are in his/her mesosystem.

Settings can also be connected by *supplemental links*, or people who also enter and participate in the same settings.

When two settings are connected by the participation of two people who have a dyadic relation, the people are said to be a *transcontextual dyad.*

Entering new settings with a person one already knows typically makes the transition easier, unless the companion doesn't help, or has difficulty entering the new setting.

Supplemental links between settings can be supportive or non-supportive of the participation and development of the person who is the primary link.

Settings can also be connected by:

- *communication* between them; and by
- the *knowledge* people in one setting have about the other.

A mesosystem can also be characterized by a *variety of relations among the settings*:

- How *similar* are the microsystems in each setting? Are the roles, relations, and activities familiar to the person entering the setting, or are they new? Are the patterns familiar?
- How *compatible* are the settings? They may be different from each other, yet still harmonious. Do the roles in one interfere with a person performing a role expected in the other setting?
- How *supportive* are the settings of each other? Do the participants in each like the participants in the other? Is there conflict, encouragement of participation in the other, or disparagement?
- What are the *attitudes* of one setting about the other? The *affect*? Do people in one setting engage in *relations* and *activities* with people in a second setting, *in third settings*? Is there reinforcement or rehearsal of activities engaged in by the person in the other setting? Do people in one help explain the experience a person has in the other? Is there common language?

Communication includes communication *between* the settings as well as communication *about* one setting within the other.

Knowledge about settings is created by participating in them, communicating with people in them, talking with people about them, reading about them, and more.

Over time, the settings and activities we engage in tend to be related to each other. When several settings, over time, encourage the development of a particular complex activity that we are motivated to continue, a "*developmental trajectory*" is established. A developmental trajectory of settings and related activities tends to underlie each important activity in a life. Developmental trajectories influence which settings we enter, and which ones we don't, as we choose those that are made available through our developing interests and skills or seek out those that will enhance those interests and skills.

Settings a person does *not* participate in may still influence development, and may be influenced by what happens in the person's mesosystem settings. Such settings and their bidirectional influences make up the person's *exosystem*.

Culture, or the macrosystem, is represented at the ecosystem level by the existence of consistencies across settings, microsystems, roles, relations, activities, and relations between settings.

As time passes, everything changes—people, places, settings, microsystems, mesosystems, exosystems, macrosystems, and ecosystems. The patterns of those changes and their effects on development make up the *chronosystem*.

APPENDIX I

Selected Works of Urie Bronfenbrenner Pertinent to Develecology

Bronfenbrenner, U. (1977). The ecology of human development in retrospect and prospect. In H. McGurk (Ed.), *Ecological Factors in Human Development* (pp. 275–286). The Netherlands: North Holland.

Bronfenbrenner, U. (1977). Lewinian space and ecological substance. *Journal of Social Issues*, 32, 513–531.

Bronfenbrenner, U. (1979). *The Ecology of Human Development: Experiments by Nature and Design*. Cambridge, MA: Harvard University Press.

Bronfenbrenner, U. (1983). The context of development and the development of context. In R. M. Lerner (Ed.), *Developmental Psychology: Historical and Philosophical Perspectives* (pp. 147–184). Hillsdale, NJ: Erlbaum.

Bronfenbrenner, U. (1984). The parent/child relationship and our changing society. In L. E. Arnold (Ed.), *Parents, Children, and Change* (pp. 45–57). Lexington, MA: Heath.

Bronfenbrenner, U. (1986). Ecology of the family as a context for human development: Research perspectives. *Developmental Psychology*, 22, 723–742.

Bronfenbrenner, U. (1986). Recent advances in research on the ecology of human development. In R. K. Silbereisen, K. Eyferth, & G. Rudinger (Eds.), *Development as Action in Context: Problem Behavior and Normal Youth Development* (pp. 287–309). New York: Springer-Verlag.

Bronfenbrenner, U. (1988). Interacting systems in human development. Research paradigms: Present and future. In N. Bolger, A. Caspi, G. Downey, & M. Moorehouse (Eds.), *Persons in Context: Developmental Processes* (pp. 25–49). New York: Cambridge University Press.

Bronfenbrenner, U. (1989). Ecological systems theory. In R. Vasta (Ed.), *Annals of Child Development, Vol. 6, Six Theories of Child Development: Revised Formulations and Current Issues* (pp. 187–249). London: JAI Press

Bronfenbrenner, U. (1990). Discovering what families do. In D. Blankenhorn, S. Bayme, & J. B. Elshtain (Eds.), *Rebuilding the Nest* (pp. 27–38). Milwaukee, WI: Family Service America.

Bronfenbrenner, U. (1993). The ecology of cognitive development: Research models and fugitive findings. In R. H. Wozniak & K. Fischer (Eds.), *Scientific Environments* (pp. 3–44). Hillsdale, NJ: Erlbaum.

Bronfenbrenner, U. (1994). Ecological models of human development. In T. Husen & T. N. Postlethwaite (Eds.), *International Encyclopedia of Education* (2nd ed., Vol. 3, pp. 1643–1647). Oxford: Pergamon/Elsevier Science.

Bronfenbrenner, U. (1995). The bioecological model from a life course perspective: Reflections of a participant observer. In P. Moen, G. H. Elder, Jr., & K. Luscher (Eds.), *Examining Lives in Context: Perspectives on the Ecology of Human Development* (pp. 599–618). Washington, DC: American Psychological Association.

Bronfenbrenner, U. (1995). Developmental ecology through space and time: A future perspective. In P. Moen, G. H. Elder, Jr., & K. Luscher (Eds.), *Examining Lives in Context: Perspectives on the Ecology of Human Development* (pp. 619–647). Washington, DC: American Psychological Association.

Bronfenbrenner, U. (1999). Environments in developmental perspective: Theoretical and operational models. In S. L. Friedman & T. D. Wachs (Eds.), *Measuring Environment across the Life Span: Emerging Methods and Concepts* (pp. 3–28). Washington, DC: American Psychological Association.

Bronfenbrenner, U. (2001). The bioecological theory of human development. In N. J. Smelser & P. B. Baltes (Eds.), *International Encyclopedia of the Social and Behavior Sciences* (Vol. 10, pp. 6963–6970). New York: Elsevier.

Bronfenbrenner, U. Ed. (2005). *Making Human Beings Human: Bioecological Perspectives on Human Development*. Thousand Oaks, CA: Sage.

Bronfenbrenner, U. & Ceci, S. J. (1993). Heredity, environment, and the question "How?" A new theoretical perspective for the 1990's. In R. Plomin & G. E. McClern (Eds.), *Nature, Nurture, and Psychology* (pp. 313–323). Washington, DC: American Psychological Association.

Bronfenbrenner, U. & Ceci, S. J. (1994). Nature-nurture reconceptualized: A bioecological model. *Psychological Review*, 101, 568–586.

Bronfenbrenner, U. & Ceci, S. J. (1994). Toward a more developmental behavioral genetics. *Social Development*, 3, 64–65.

Bronfenbrenner, U., Ceci, S. J., & Baker-Sennett, J. (1994). Cognition in and out of context: A tale of two paradigms. In M. Rutter & D. F. Hay (Eds.), *Development through Life: A Handbook for Clinicians* (pp. 239–259). Oxford: Blackwell.

Bronfenbrenner, U., Ceci, S. J., & Baker-Sennett, J. (1994). Psychometric and everyday intelligence: Synonyms, antonyms, and anonyms. In M. Rutter & D. F. Hay (Eds.), *Development through Life: A Handbook for Clinicians* (pp. 260–283). Oxford: Blackwell.

Bronfenbrenner, U. & Crouter, A. C. (1983). The evolution of environmental models in developmental research. In W. Kessen (Series Ed.) & P. H. Mussen (Vol. Ed.), *Handbook of Child Psychology: Vol. 1. History, Theory, and Methods* (4th ed., pp. 357–414). New York: Wiley.

Bronfenbrenner, U., & Evans, G. W. (2000). Developmental science in the 21st century: Emerging questions, theoretical models, research designs and empirical findings. *Social Development*, 9(1), 115–125.

Bronfenbrenner, U., McClelland, P., Wethington, E., Moen, P., & Ceci, S. J. (1996). *The State of Americans: This Generation and the Next*. New York: Free Press.

Bronfenbrenner, U., Moen, P. & Garbarino, J. (1984). Child, family and community. In R. D. Parke (Ed.), *Review of Child Development Research: The Family* (Vol. 7, pp. 283–328). Chicago: University of Chicago.

Bronfenbrenner, U. & Morris, P. A. (1998). The ecology of developmental processes. In R. Lerner (Series Ed.) & W. Damon (Vol. Ed.), *Handbook of Child Psychology: Vol. 1. Theory* (5th ed., pp. 993–1028). New York: Wiley.

Bronfenbrenner, U. & Neville, P. R. (1994). America's children and families: An international perspective. In S. L. Kagan & B. Weissbourd (Eds.), *Putting Families First* (pp. 3–27). San Francisco: Jossey-Bass.

Bronfenbrenner, U. & Weiss, H. (1983). Beyond policies without people: An ecological perspective on child and family policy. In E. F. Zigler, S. L. Kagan, & E. Klugman (Eds.), *Children, Families, and Government* (pp. 393–414). New York: Cambridge University Press.

APPENDIX II

Directory of Bronfenbrenner's Definitions, Propositions, and Hypotheses in Urie Bronfenbrenner, *The Ecology of Human Development* (Cambridge, MA: Harvard University Press, 1979)

Item	Page	Topic
DEFINITION 1	p. 21	**ecology of human development**
		Revised in Bronfenbrenner (1989), p. 188
DEFINITION 2	p. 22	**Microsystem**
		Revised in Bronfenbrenner (1989), p. 227
DEFINITION 3	p. 25	**Mesosystem**
		Revised in Bronfenbrenner (1989), p. 227
DEFINITION 4	p. 25	**Exosystem**
		Revised in Bronfenbrenner (1994), p. 1645
DEFINITION 5	p. 26	**Macrosystem**
		Revised in Bronfenbrenner (1989), p. 228
DEFINITION 6	p. 26	**ecological transition**
DEFINITION 7	p. 27	**human development**
DEFINITION 8	p. 29	**ecological validity** in research
DEFINITION 9	p. 35	**developmental validity.**
DEFINITION 10	p. 36	**ecological experiment**
DEFINITION 11	p. 41	**transforming experiment**
DEFINITION 12	p. 45	**molar activity**
DEFINITION 13	p. 56	**relation**
	p. 56	**dyad**
	p. 56	**observational dyad**
	pp. 56–57	**joint activity dyad**
	p. 58	**primary dyad**

continued

Item	Page	Topic
DEFINITION 14	p. 85	**role**
		chronosystem added in Bronfenbrenner (1994), p. 1646
PROPOSITION A	p. 41	ecological research, in systems terms
PROPOSITION B	p. 55	**developmental status**
PROPOSITION C	p. 65	change in dyad
PROPOSITION D	p. 66	full interpersonal system
PROPOSITION E	p. 68	**second-order effect**
PROPOSITION F	p. 109	different kinds of settings
PROPOSITION G	p. 121	ecologically valid setting for research
PROPOSITION G'	p. 125	ecologically valid setting and subject's experience
PROPOSITION H	p. 183	different settings, different developmental effects, reflect ecological differences
HYPOTHESIS 1	p. 55	**molar activities in development**
HYPOTHESIS 2	p. 59	observational dyads transformed into joint activity dyads
HYPOTHESIS 3	p. 59	joint activity dyads transformed into primary dyads
HYPOTHESIS 4	p. 59	developmental impact of dyad greater if reciprocity, mutuality of positive feeling, and shift of power toward developing person
HYPOTHESIS 5	pp. 59–60	learning facilitated in context of joint activity dyad
HYPOTHESIS 6	p. 60	learning enhanced in context of primary dyad characterized by mutuality of positive feeling
HYPOTHESIS 7	60	developmental dyad
HYPOTHESIS 8	p. 77	dyad affected by other dyadic relationships with third parties
HYPOTHESIS 9	p. 92	placement of person in a role evokes consistent expectations associated with that role
HYPOTHESIS 10	p. 92	role well established in the society with broad consensus about expectations
HYPOTHESIS 11	p. 92	degree of power for a given role
HYPOTHESIS 12	p. 94	behavior in accord with a given role and existence of other roles associated with the role
HYPOTHESIS 13	p. 101	social roles compatible with the given expectations
HYPOTHESIS 14	p. 104	development facilitated through interaction with variety of roles and participation in broad role repertoire

Item	Page	Topic
HYPOTHESIS 15	p. 143	environment damaging when few possibilities for child–caretaker interaction in a variety of activities, and restricted locomotion and few objects for activity
HYPOTHESIS 16	p. 143	disruptive impact of impoverished environment greatest for children separated from parent in second half year
HYPOTHESIS 17	p. 144	conditions to avert or reverse effects of institutionalization
HYPOTHESIS 18	p. 150	deleterious effects of impoverished environment decrease with age of child upon entry
HYPOTHESIS 19	p. 163	developmental potential of setting enhanced if enables and motivates complex molar activities, reciprocal interaction, and primary dyadic relationships
HYPOTHESIS 20	p. 201	effects of exposure to group settings in early childhood reflected in molar activities engaged in by the child and behavior and relations toward adults and peers.
HYPOTHESIS 21	p. 202	group settings for young children
HYPOTHESIS 22	p. 202	caregivers or preschool teachers
HYPOTHESIS 23	p. 203	effects of early all day group care include egocentric, aggressive, antisocial behavior through childhood into adolescence, particularly for boys, especially if society encourages individualism, aggression and independence in children's groups, especially by boys
HYPOTHESIS 24	p. 203	variety and complexity of molar activities
HYPOTHESIS 25	p. 204	relations and roles engaged in by child in daycare or preschool setting affect nature and complexity of roles and relations initiated or entered into in other settings
HYPOTHESIS 26	p. 204	developmental potential of a daycare or preschool setting
	p. 209	**multisetting participation**
	p. 210	**intersetting communications**
	p. 210	**intersetting knowledge**
HYPOTHESIS 27	p. 211	developmental potential of setting in mesosystem enhanced if initial transition into setting not made alone
HYPOTHESIS 28	p. 212	the developmental potential of settings in a mesosystem is enhanced if the role demands in the different settings are compatible and if the roles, activities, and

continued

Item	Page	Topic
HYPOTHESIS 45	p. 256	number of links connecting to settings of power.
HYPOTHESIS 46	p. 282	Revised by Shelton, this volume responsible, task-oriented activities with adults other than parents
HYPOTHESIS 47	pp. 284–285	**developmental trajectories**
HYPOTHESIS 48	p. 286	**primary transition** and sleeper effects
HYPOTHESIS 49	p. 288	psychological growth and opportunities to enter settings
HYPOTHESIS 50	p. 288	transition from primary setting

INDEX

Page numbers in *italics* denote figures.